It's All BS!
We're All Wrong,
and You're All Right!

Jason Richardson PsyD., MBA

Rob Irwin PhD

Acknowledgements

With so many people, experiences, and good fortune, it's difficult to express all the gratitude and obligation I have. Like a favorite movie, the ensemble cast of characters and behind-the-scenes crew is unmatched and award winning. The soundtrack contains hit after hit, with every song eliciting the exact mood, tempo, and emotion of the moment. I live and work with my favorite people. And it's not their talents that I am indebted to; it's the relationships themselves.

Pushed, pulled, carried, drafted, educated, raced, familied, friended, challenged, lifted, and gifted—all of the moments serve their purpose. All of my favorite people with me wherever I go:

Dr. Rob Irwin – What an IDEAL way to keep the story going! Thank you for sharing and shedding your spotlight.

Lou (Dad): Work until the work is through, right? I'll always run toward you and walk away slowly.

Halé, Greyson, Decklen: I know I can be a bit "rich" at times. Thank you for your grace. And yes, Grey, I, too, often wonder, "How could mom marry that guy?"

Sean, Marcus, Anthony, Craig (The MMG): Okay, gentlemen . . . What's good?

The BMX world: Thank you for the metaphor. A lifetime within a lifetime on an infinite continuum; I hope all of our memories are better than the rides! #WELLthCycle

Foreword

I have been given so many shots in life that it never occurred to me not to take my own. As you read (or listen to) the words in this book, you should know that I am an unlikely champion—both *in* my life and *for* your life. Had these shots never been given or taken, I would probably not be a champion.

Moments are what we aim for—being crowned champion, accepting the diploma, watching your child take his or her first steps. Indelible time stamps in our minds, and fleeting just the same. The moment there's a slight shift in perspective or a nudge in a particular direction is all it takes to experience exponential gains down the road.

And it really does just take moments!

Introduction: Winning the Human Race

Being a winner in life extends beyond the scoreboard, the track, and the field. Gem-encrusted championship rings are sold on eBay by ring holders who found themselves either broke, in legal trouble, or just plain desperate. If only they applied the same mindset to their off-the-field life as they did to their game. If only they embraced the same belief system (hereafter referred to as "B.S.") they held when they were on the field of play. If only they recognized the game was not confined to the minutes on the shot clock or the seconds between the start and finish line. It's time we expand our understanding of winning the game from four quarters or two halves to a period that spans a lifetime. Make no mistake, we're all playing the long game whether we like it or not, whether we know it or not, whether we want to or not. In the game of life, anybody can win, but not everyone is a winner or believes they are!

The beliefs we have about who we are, what is possible, and what we are capable of create the lens through which we see the world. This lens can skew or enhance our view of the field (proverbial or otherwise) on which we play. In either case, our view of the field affects our play, and our play determines the results.

The B.S. we embrace directly affects whether we play big or play small. Our beliefs can be global and/or specific to our work, play, and life. Sometimes, however, those beliefs are at odds. Think of the confident star quarterback who struggles with academics. For him, learning every detail of a complex playbook is easy because it's tied to a different B.S. than remembering the periodic table of elements. The reason so many pro athletes have trouble transitioning out of athletics and into the "real world" is due to the same reason our star quarterback is failing chemistry. If he believes he is just a football player, then life after football looks grim. If he sees himself as a "dumb jock," he will be looking for someone to take tests for him—forever. However, these are nothing but beliefs. Unfortunately, for our QB, belief systems, it turns out, are the source of our feelings, actions, and results.

Athletes are not alone. There's a bit of Clark Kent and Superman in all of us.

So, welcome to the human race. Hopefully, you plan on winning it! This is where the story gets interesting.

Chapter 1

You've Been Told NO More
Than You Know.

One of the perks of being a psychologist is that everyone tells you everything, eventually! Hearing that Mr. X is cheating on Mrs. X is unfortunate. It's also more than a bit clichéd when you find out Mr. X cheated with the nanny or Mrs. X's best friend. Those are the big issues: cheating spouses, depression, anxiety, eating disorders, ADHD, etc. Everyone more or less knows the reasons why they're on the couch if they are dealing with one of these issues in their lives. What is peculiar and what often raises red flags are the things people tend to casually breeze over during their session:

Client: "Yeah, back when I was a drug dealer . . ." or, "She called the cops on me but . . ."

Me: "Pardon me. What did you just say? Can we press rewind?"

What is of particular interest is the more nuanced dialogue disguised as common sense. These clichés are often more dubious than we think, warranting, at the very least, a cautionary yellow flag:

"You need a fallback plan." *Plan B sucks!*

"Don't put all your eggs in one basket." *Easter egg hunting will never be the same.*

"You can't have your cake and eat it, too!" *Stale cake doesn't do anyone good.*

"Not everybody will (or can) become a _____." *If not you, then who?*

Part of the reason for waving the yellow caution flag on these clichés lays in their ubiquity and that the ubiquitous is generally taken for granted or accepted as fact. Like a Starbucks in every strip mall or the fact that the Lululemon store is almost always placed within eyeshot of the Apple Store. What we assume we are taking at face value still communicates a deeper message.

The four sayings above are spoken as if "that's just the

way it is" and they're understood as if they are not to be questioned. Many of us subconsciously sabotage our inclination toward the initial thing we want to do because these clichés have hidden back doors built into them—a way out when the going gets tough.

The good news is this: you are primed for an amazing amount of optimism. How else would you come up with such grand ideas in the first place? The irony? Our friends, parents, and school counselors say such things out of good intention, so we don't get our hopes up too much. The problem is[1] that, on your way to doing or becoming what you want in life, you have been told N-O more times than you can k-n-o-w[2] and, unfortunately, in more ways than you would expect.

The other day I heard a kid tell his dad that he wanted to be a pro athlete, and the first thing that came out of the parent's mouth was, "Well son, that means you've got to practice a lot and study real hard—not everyone makes it to the pros." At that point I thought to myself, "Why on earth would this kid want to continue down that path? How is this motivating? Especially to a kid." Somewhere between Daniel Coyle's book, *The Talent Code*, and anything Malcolm Gladwell has written, we feel it's necessary to impress upon our younger protégés, children, or

---

[1] This statement comes up later and is addressed more fully. I am purposely being tongue in cheek by using it.
[2] Urban legend has it that UCLA conducted a study finding the average toddler hears the word "No" 400 times a day.

mentees, just how much work it takes to achieve. But does a ten-year-old need to know it takes 10,000 hours to gain mastery in a subject?[3] Shouldn't we just say to such a bright-eyed boy, "Cool, let's make it happen!"

The Fallback Plan. If the goal is singular, contingency plans make sense. For instance, assume an athlete has a singular goal of becoming an Olympic medalist. Her performance plan based on the goal most likely includes what events to attend, how to get there, the requirements to make her Olympic team, and the physical and mental preparation to be in top form for those events—in addition to being medal-capable once at the Games. Since there are many moving parts in such a program, her performance plan would include contingencies for challenges that may arise on her way to Gold, such as illness, injury, missing an event, etc. The fallback plan is developed to offset risks that have a negative impact on meeting the objective. In general, a fallback plan is an "alternative" used in case a certain approach fails.[4] Notice that the GOAL is still the same, even once the fallback plan needs to be put into action—here, the fallback plan is a different route to the same end.

---

[3] Some would say the 10,000 hour rule "simply does not exist." http://www.smithsonianmag.com/smart-news/10000-hour-rule-not-real-180952410/?no-ist
[4] http://www.projectmanagementquestions.com/707/what-is-a-fallback-plan

Why Plan B Sucks[5] (still talking about fallback plans). When a kid says, "I want to go the Super Bowl one day, but everyone tells me I need a fallback plan," is VERY different from what was just described above. Notice, there are now two different goals. One is clear; the other *might* be clear, but it also represents a different end. You are not fully to blame for thinking you need a fallback plan, by the way. Your parents and friends are also not (fully) at fault for suggesting you "have to be realistic." This version of the fallback plan, the one many of us have been told, implies defeat. Not loss, but defeat. Loss is dynamic, momentary, and educational. Defeat is loss with the lack of will to get back up. It's the loss of your internal drive.[6] The reason Plan B is debilitating is that it's something OTHER than what you initially set out to do.

Candidly, I played it both ways at the onset of my professional athletic career. For my parents, continuing with school throughout my racing days was my fallback plan. For me, I always wanted to go to college anyway, and there was no sense in putting education on hold just because of my athletic endeavors. After my first round in graduate school, I realized that school and sport can be part of the same plan. It wasn't about making it as a pro. It was about being a pro with advanced degrees, thus setting myself up for ongoing success.

---

[5] "Work on your dreams, not your boss'"
www.planbsucksbook.com/book

[6] We look at loss versus defeat much as many distinguish between listening and hearing. They can mean the same thing, but one implies a deeper level. Defeat implies a deeper level of loss.

You are not wrong for thinking you need a fallback plan. You just want the right kind of fallback plan.

Easter Egg Hunting. This is a tricky one because it depends on the basket. Where are you placing your eggs? Are they in someone else's basket, or are you putting them in your own? If you are putting them in someone else's basket, then move to reallocate or diversify. If it's in your basket, why not "double-down" on yourself? Going to the races and betting on a horse might be risky. And because it's risky, you probably don't want to bet your full bankroll on any one horse. Conventional wisdom says the smart play is to place different bets on different horses, spreading your risk and maximizing opportunities to win, place, or show. Presuming you don't have unlimited funds and you're just out to have a good time at the track, this strategy makes sense. There's another side of that truth, however: just as you minimize losses based on the "distribution of risk" strategy, you also minimize your return if one of those horses comes in. You lose little, but you also win little.

Now, here's the real issue: when playing the ponies, you are also playing another person's game. Even if you bet everything on one horse, you still don't have a horse in the race because you most likely don't own the horse! The owners, however, do have a horse or several in the race, and those owners are all-in. They have hundreds of thousands, possibly millions, of dollars invested in their game. The trainers are all-in. The jockeys are all-in. Those folks' eggs are all in one basket because

15

they own the basket! The owners are winning despite the horse's results.[7] They have more than just money invested. Time, effort, and emotion are the other eggs that lay in their basket. An owner goes in knowing that losses are inevitable. Their "fallback plan" is to win eventually, and win big. Whether racing, breeding, or trading, profits can be made before and after the race is run but only for the owner of the basket.

What are you betting on when you enter a race? If you find yourself in more than one race—say sports and school, a job and a start-up, school and a job—are you betting on the event? Or are you betting on yourself? Betting on the event is playing the odds, and playing the odds makes you a gambler. Betting on yourself makes you an investor. And, let's face it: the best investors know something everyone else doesn't. What is it you know about yourself and your capabilities that no one else knows? If you don't know something about yourself, are you willing to pay to find out? Both require investment.

Eating Your Cake. Because we are so far removed from the inception of this cliché, most people tend to think, "Well, isn't that the point of cake? To eat it?" In all fairness, the statement goes a bit deeper. Basically, eating the cake you have will result in no longer having any cake, because it's gone— you ate it. Wisdom is sometimes lost when things are taken at face value. Unfortunately, as wise as "You can't have your cake and

---

[7] Rao, Jessica. "Horses Are An Investment You Can Ride" http://www.cnbc.com/id/39342161#

eat it too!" may have started out to be, it has evolved into a statement that now has little meaning beyond, "You can't!" or, "You can't have it both ways."

Every time I go the fridge or kitchen to get a piece of fruit, I always choose the *best* one. However, this practice gives me pause—in choosing the best apple from the bunch, technically my selection options get worse every time I go back. Yet, this is not my experience. I enjoy my apple every time because on that day I got the best of the bunch. It doesn't matter that the apple I chose yesterday may have been better than the one I am choosing today. If I go to the fruit bowl thinking my choice of apples is worse today than yesterday, I will most likely not be satisfied with my choice. If I save what I think to be the best of the bunch for last, I run the risk of losing out on that choice to someone else or having that perfect apple go bad, thus never getting to experience the best of the bunch.

Exercising restraint by holding off on the immediate, smaller reward now for the larger outcome later is good when investing time, money, and effort. The question we all must face is "When do we collect the return on those investments?" Perishable items should be enjoyed when they are ripe for the picking. Most everything we have materially only lasts temporarily. Some things last longer, keep better, and are worth saving. Other things are meant for enjoyment in the moment. Stating it bluntly, even things that last your entire lifetime expire when you do because your time here is finite. It really isn't about the cake anyway. It's about how limited thinking acts to limit our experiences.

One afternoon, I walked a client to the parking lot after our meeting. I joked he was driving my favorite car.[8] He stopped walking, turned to face me, and started in on a story:

"When I started making money, I bought my dream car. I was careful not to drive it too much; I loved driving it but was always uneasy about putting too many miles on the odometer."

Within a year of buying it, he and his wife found out they would be having their first child, and the two-seater was traded in for a more family-friendly vehicle.

"You know, Doc, I was okay with letting the car go, but my biggest regret was that I didn't drive it enough! Hell, if I wanted that car today, I'd be paying more money for an older car with more miles!"

I asked him if he is enjoying his current car.

"Cars are meant to be driven, not feather dusted in some garage once a week. I drive this thing every chance I get! I find myself making up reasons to run an errand. I could care less about the mileage."

I smiled and said, "Seems like you value the experience more than the item."

---

[8] I actually have several favorites! If we ever meet one day, I'd love to talk cars.

"That's right, Doc! Who says you can't have your cake and eat it too?!"

I am not suggesting people use their Civil War coin collection to buy a pack of gum. In the spirit of good manners, I hope you save the last piece of fruit or cake for your mom or dad, husband, or wife.

The driving force of this section is about wrapping your brain around the possibilities, known and unforeseen. If you believe "I can't have my cake and eat it too," you are essentially saying you can only go so far, that you are somehow limited. That limiting mentality, whether it is specific to a small facet of your life or part of an overarching belief system, limits your potential. There are already plenty of natural limits in the world. There is no need to add the self-imposed variety.

At every point in human existence, someone somewhere decided to take that bite of cake. If you don't eat your cake, simply for the sake of keeping it whole, all you'll end up with is stale cake. It will cease to be as beautiful as it once was because it's a perishable item. You will never experience the satisfaction and pleasure it might bring. The potential within you IS that cake, by the way! Most importantly, if you don't eat your cake, it's because you choose not to, not because you can't.

If Not You, Then Who? Our world is full of resources, natural and otherwise. We have come to know those resources are limited. Oil, water, trees, and air all must be protected and

19

conserved because they are either in short or uncertain supply, or their quality is in decline. Because of this, we pay dearly for the use of those resources.

Unfortunately, the economic principle of "limited resources" has bled into our views on what may be possible for us out there in the world. The "Occupy Movement" of 2011, in part, put forth the message, "Since you have so much, I am forced to settle for less."[9] What was unsettling about the Occupy Movement was the sheer number of people demonstrating a belief in improbability rather than possibility. Were their dreams no longer available to them? Are their dreams now somehow more difficult to achieve? Or is it a case of their subjective lives not meeting their own expectations and supposed entitlements?

If so, how is it that people in the same peer groups regularly beat the odds and succeeded on a massive scale? Zuckerberg, 29 (Facebook), Muskovitz, 29 (Facebook), Houston, 30 (DropBox), Baba, 36 (Colopl), Dorsey 37 (Twitter), Holmes, 30 (Theranos)? We cannot know the full range of each individual's personal beliefs, but a good wager can be placed on the entrepreneurs' beliefs in what was possible for them and for the world. They became successful despite student debt or Wall Street's greed. They "occupy" Wall Street too, just in a different way than those doing the protesting.

---

[9] http://en.wikipedia.org/wiki/Occupy_Wall_Street

Recently, there was an article about a yacht that sank on launch day. What immediately came to mind as I began to read the article was, "I'll bet there are a bunch of people "hating on" the ship owners in the comments section."[10] It was no surprise that my bet with myself paid off as I scrolled through a thick page of the unfortunately typical "Serves them right" type of comments. My momentary validation of being right was interrupted by a couple of troublesome questions:

1) Why do we cast aspersions on others for being wealthy (or poor, for that matter)?

2) Why was it my first instinct to think this would be the case?"

It wasn't long ago that, upon hearing such a story, the majority of people would show some level of compassion for those involved or at least understand this was a misfortune not only for the owner, but also for all those who worked to design and build the boat. Since when did it become socially acceptable to say, "Serves them right?" Since when did it become okay to even say, "They have insurance, it won't affect them?" Who are the "they" or "them" anyway? That mindset sounds eerily familiar to the "Let them eat cake" mentality, just on the other end of the continuum.[11]

---

[10] To be fair, there were also posts by other readers lambasting those reveling in the sinking yacht.

[11] This famous quote is commonly misattributed to Marie Antoinette, who was only eight years of age when she supposedly said it. Unbeknownst to most, she actually "donated generously" to charity.

There was a time when people celebrated each other's good fortune. Seeing a buddy, or even a stranger, achieve a dream made us want to go after our dreams. It was an inspiration, not an occasion for sour grapes. If we are following social or traditional media, we see an "us vs. them" theme in many stories and threads. Unfortunately, the evidence suggests there are a growing number of people who revel in the misfortune of others, in their "epic fails." If those numbers aren't growing, they at least seem to be getting more play. Hardened newsmen wept when the Hindenburg went down and when JFK was shot and killed. A luxury blimp falling from the sky in flames is not a fail. It was a tragedy, regardless of how privileged those involved may have been. How did it become such a "zero-sum game" that someone else's success means we are somehow losing?

Your neighbor getting a new car, a friend landing his dream job, and a former coworker's start-up going public means good things ARE possible—not unobtainable. In a world of "limited resources," one might think there is only so much of the pie to go around, so "you'd better get your sliver." In a world of unlimited possibilities, it's about baking bigger and better pies. People pushing forward actually expand our resources. Economic pundits say wealth is created. That statement is incomplete. Wealth is created, but it is also earned and, yes,

---

http://www.history.com/news/ask-history/did-marie-antoinette-really-say-let-them-eat-cake

inherited—if not by birthright, then definitely through workright!

Yes, not everyone will become a yacht owner, Olympic medalist, or Nobel Prize winner. These are awards that only a small percentage of people each generation will earn. There are people, like those who commented on the yacht article, who are all too happy to tell you how improbable your goals, wants, and dreams may be. The sad part is you won't likely hear the doubt coming solely from the antagonists. It sometimes comes from the people who care about you the most. They don't want to see you discouraged, see you struggle, or see you waste your time with something impractical or "unrealistic." It's your loved ones' way of saying, "Be careful" or "I've got to make sure this kid can make a living for himself; he can't live here forever!" To be fair, it's not doubt that is coming from your loved ones—it's care, even though it's based in fear. Nonetheless, the "problems" with an idea seem to be pointed out more than the solutions.

The problem with saying "the problem is" is it rules things out rather than rules things in. Someone might say, "The problem with wanting to be a professional athlete is the chance of injury." Or, "The problem with attending graduate school is the cost. What is it going to DO for you?" Or maybe, "The problem with running for president is the dirty politics." You get the idea. But what worthwhile things in life are totally problem free? Maybe "the problem" is not a problem at all. Maybe those perceived problems are merely steps along the

obstertunities

way. There are a multitude of individuals, teams, and enterprises in this world advancing in their endeavors despite the so-called problems associated with their respective goals. What if that somebody were you?

It's difficult to challenge yourself. It's difficult to look at the evidence and say something's not true. Michael Jordan used to win often and win big. Manning, any Manning you choose, wins often and wins big. But, at some point someone says, "Why not me?" This was the sentiment of Russell Wilson, the Seattle Seahawks quarterback, during the run-up to his 2013 Super Bowl win. His belief was within himself and his team. He was most likely saying, "I (We) can do this!"

Judging by his demeanor and the way he spoke, it was apparent he respected his competitors—it was not about taking anything away from them. Wilson's respect for the competition probably helped him because he knew exactly what and with whom he was dealing. He was playing against the best! It just didn't matter, because he believed he and his team were the best, too!

Many of us make the mistake of thinking the best is a "one-and-only" condition. Seth Godin, author of *The Dip*, reminds us that the best can include more than one in any given set.[12] There is a range of best. Pick any Hall of Fame and you'll find such a range of best, not just a sole inductee. If you concede

---

[12] Godin, Seth. *The Dip*

that someone else is the best, at the expense of your output, then you definitely won't rise to the top. The best compete against the best. Coke and Pepsi share a space. Olympians, world champions, and industry leaders share a space. The Hall of Fame of anything is a shared space!

We often make the mistake of thinking our competitors want us to lose, which is not necessarily true. Most of the time, they just want to win too! They are not "taking it" from you, especially if you never had it in the first place. They are getting it for themselves, and YOU have the opportunity to get it for yourself. Yes, not everyone will become president or sell their start-up for billions. Hopefully, you are not "everyone." By the way, not everyone wants to become president or create the next Uber, so the odds are tipped in your favor if that's your dream. Take a minute to consider who is telling you NO now.

Chapter 2

The Honest Lie

"Your BeLIEf Creates The Foundation For The FACTs."

Most new information introduced to your brain begins as a lie. Think of a little baby enthralled with a game of peekaboo. She's laughing and smiling away because she cannot believe how you can disappear and then all of a sudden reappear! To a baby, hiding behind the chair means you are gone. More specifically, it means only the chair is there. The infant does not yet comprehend that you are actually behind the object. That baby is saying, "No way! You were there, and then all I saw was the chair . . . and now you're back! How did you do that?"

Despite your grasp of object permanence[13], our brains are rather infantile when new concepts are introduced. Yet, given enough evidence over time, your brain begins to accept new information. That new information becomes your truth. Why do you think magicians are so captivating and entertaining? They seem to defy our known world by playing off of our beliefs. Intellectually, you know the magician is tricking you. Yet you are still willing to suspend your disbelief. Of course, that's why it's entertaining—the defiance of what the mind accepts as truth: "Did you see that? It was unbelievable!" Obviously, there's a trick to the trick, and when you learn what's actually behind the curtain, it ceases to have the same entertainment value.

There is a lie inside every beLIEf, both literally and figuratively. Magicians bank on this concept for their success![14] The magician may not be affecting reality in a raw sense, but he is definitely affecting what you perceive to be reality—your "truth." Let's sit with that for a moment. We know full well what we're seeing is an illusion, but we are still in disbelief and entertained when the rabbit is pulled from the hat. How is it we can intellectually know something: "The magician is going to trick me" and still be in shock when he does exactly what we

---

[13] Piaget, J.—The ability of a child to understand that objects exist even if they cannot directly be sensed. Think of the phrase "out of sight, out of mind."

[14] http://www.cirquedusoleil.com/en/shows/believe/default.aspx

expect? The answer lies in our beliefs and our mostly unionized brain circuitry. In other words, your beliefs are so deeply rooted about even the most unassuming and unthreatening things that your intellectual capacity becomes overridden by the "union demand" to support the deeply held belief. There are other things that come into play. Maybe it's a twist on the old classic "thwarting your expectations." Maybe the trick elicits your own magical thinking? That part of you that is secretly thinking, "Something else is out there." Either way, the lack of evidence tells your union to say, "Hell no, we won't go!" It's just like a factory closing down because of a strike, though not nearly as serious. The superstar headliners defy much bigger or deeply held beliefs, such as gravity, death, etc., which is why David Blain and Chris Angel hold our attention even if we are just casually flipping through the channels. They give us the heebie-jeebies on a neurological level.

The brain's most important function is to keep you alive. After we get past food, clothing, shelter, and safety, the definition of survival becomes very subjective. The subjective nature of survival has to do with how we perceive that the world perceives us. Daniel Kahneman states it quite well in his book, *Thinking Fast and Thinking Slow*: "Organisms that placed more urgency on avoiding threats than they did on maximizing opportunities were more likely to pass on their genes. So over time, the prospect of losses has become a more powerful motivator on your behavior than the promise of gains."[15] For the brain, it's all about safety. Feel free to substitute the word safety for "comfort" or "familiarity."

In the developed world, the hungry do not starve, many below the poverty line have big screen televisions and smartphones, and the hippies of the 1960s and 1970s are now the millionaire establishment, at least in the Bay Area![16] Political discourse aside, survival is subjective because our basic needs are already met. Therefore, your brain goes to work on keeping you safe physically, emotionally, psychologically, and socially. This is where, when, and how the beLIEf is perpetuated. In sports, business, and Southern California, the most fragile thing the brain protects is our egos.

[15] Kahneman, Daniel. *Thinking Fast and Slow*.
[16] I know I'm going to take some hits for that one!

Chapter 3

Raw Data vs. Interpreted Data

"The magician may not be affecting reality in a raw sense but is definitely affecting what you perceive to be reality—your "truth."

You're watching the big game. Heck, maybe you're at the big game sitting in one of the best seats in the house. Your friends are watching the game, too. One of your buddies happens to be in another section of the stadium, and he always roots against your team. The rest of your crew is watching on TV. All is good until the official makes a "suspect" call. They show the replay on the big screen, and you're still in disbelief.

Sure, you want your team to win, but the call isn't bad because it doesn't favor your team. The call is bad because it's wrong. You were sitting right there when it happened; you saw it with your own eyes! "How could the referee be so blind? The ball was clearly in!" Now your phone starts to blow up, and you're immersed in a heated debate via group text:

You: "The ball was in!"

Marcus: "No way. The ball was out!"

Sean: "C'mon man, I know what I saw . . ."

Anthony: "Dude! I'm *AT* the game. I think my view is better than yours."

Craig: "What are you talking about? They've replayed it a hundred times on TV. I'm pretty sure the ref got it right."

Anthony: "Looked like a good call to me. Don't get mad 'cuz your team is losing!"

Who's right? Since this book started with a list of clichés, let's employ one more to drive home a point: There are three sides to every story: your version, my version, and the truth!

In the example above, each person has his or her own version of events—his own truth. One guy is watching it on TV, and he can never really pause it at the right moment. Either it's one frame too early or one frame late, but his DVR shows him what he wants to see anyway. The other guy is AT the game and seated in the mezzanine. He thinks HE has the best vantage point. You have prime seats at field level, right in the heart of it all. Finally, there's the referee running with and among the players—the guy who actually made the call.

The argument is not really about being "in" or "out" on the field. The argument is about defending what you think to be the case: "my perception is better than your perception." Everyone, by the way, has obstructed views. How can a guy in the nosebleed section of the stadium see everything? Your friend watching at home is at the mercy of the TV director in the trailer showing what HE perceives to be the best angle. You may have great seats, but you're competing with the people in front of you to see the field. Are you watching the Jumbotron or looking at the field when the players are in a certain position? We could argue the referee has the best view, but he is human too and doesn't have the luxury of the box seats, the DVR, or the Jumbotron. Despite each person's respective vantage point, everyone is acting on interpreted data. How many beers did you have during the game, by the way?

What you see may not actually be happening. Just like "what is said may not be heard." We make decisions and act on representations of the truth. Our biases often get in the way of discerning what actually happens in reality. Our place, station, experiences, wants, and beliefs determine bias. How is it that midwestern states are really farther east than they are in the middle? Why is a person from Pakistan considered Asian to Europeans but Middle Eastern in the United States? Why did the house you grew up in seem so big then and so small now? Our biases are much like the mirrors in the fun house at the fair. The distortion is much more subtle, but our reaction to those reflections may not be so subtle.

Truth is, the ball was in, out, or on the line. Raw data does exist in the world. The house you grew up in had a specific square footage. Unless it was demolished or renovated, it still occupies the same amount of space. Ohio is still located west of

Pennsylvania and east of Indiana. What affects these facts is our juxtaposition to them.

We may never know what is true in the raw sense. Does that mean we stop playing or participating? No, it means we learn to understand that the game is bigger than what is happening on the field of play. The field of play is tinted by our biases, and our biases are part of the field of play. We are part of the game itself even if we don't think we're playing. The seats we have, the vantage point we take, the good calls, the bad calls—along with the overpriced beer—are all part of the experience.

All judged events are fixed. Well . . . not really. It's more like we (as well as the judges) attach our "fixations" to those events. One would think racing or ball sports are more clear-cut. However, those officiating the game render their judgments based on their interpretations of the rules and, yes, what they see or believe they saw. In sports and in life, quite frankly, many things boil down to judgment calls.

What about the concept of the law itself? The tragedy in Ferguson, Missouri during the Summer/Fall of 2014 has many layers and illustrates just how deeply our individual vantage point dictates how we move about the world.[17] **Regardless of your opinion, based on what you know about the case, ask yourself what other possible outcomes might**

---

[17] http://www.nytimes.com/interactive/2014/08/13/us/ferguson-missouri-town-under-siege-after-police-shooting.html

there have been IF those involved were more aware of their own biases? Yet, it was precisely each individual's vantage point, his or her belief in their respective interpretation of the data that prompted the misfortune for the young man, the cop, the families, the town, and a nation.

Now ask yourself this: When you are in an argument (or competition), do you want to be right? Or do you want to win? There's a difference. Being right doesn't always make us winners, and winners are not always in the right.

Chapter 4

We're All Black Sheep?

"What you see may not actually be happening. Just like 'what is said may not be heard.' We make decisions and act on representations of the truth. Our biases often get in the way of discerning what actually happens in reality. Our place, station, experiences, wants, and beliefs determine bias."

How can two people who grow up in the same house under the same conditions, with the same parents, end up so different?

Two brothers born only two years apart: one is CEO of a large corporation, and the other prefers to live life "off the grid" as an artist. When they were children, their basic needs were equally met: they each had a roof over their heads, clothes on their backs, and happily married parents.

As most kids do, both had their share of struggles and growing pains, and each earned his proverbial social, religious, and familial rites of passage. Given their shared background and environment, most would think they both would have taken similar paths in their choices of career, family, and friends. Yet they matured into two profoundly different adults.

Though they were seemingly cut from the same cloth, they both learned to subjectively survive in different ways: The older brother had no choice but to deal with first-time parents, while the younger brother was born to parents who had already been parents. The older brother grew up believing he had to be responsible. "Look out for your younger brother." "Help him with his homework." "You should be more careful because you know your little brother looks up to you!" The younger brother grew up watching the older brother make mistakes. He had the luxury of seeing someone else "do it first." The older brother dealt with more ambiguity and chaos. The younger brother's experience was that of order and a set of rules based on the parent's experience with their first son.

Is it any wonder that both boys ended up taking different paths as adults? The older boy was first. His well-intentioned parents were figuring it out as they went along. He had no choice but to deal with parents experiencing every scenario for the first time. His only examples were other kids in the neighborhood and what he saw on television. The younger boy always had more than an example, he had a benchmark—

his older brother. The younger brother could always look directly to someone sharing the same room, parents, and genes, and think to himself, "I'm not doing that!" or "I like the way he does that!"

After having their first child, the parents couldn't help but use what they learned from the first to create boundaries for the second. If the younger brother got into trouble, the parents were less reactive and more responsive. So you have two boys in the same house, with the same parents, with vastly different personal experiences. Their birth order, inherent abilities, looks, features, and respective temperaments[18] all contributed to the differences in the way they see the world and the way the world sees them. Because each boy's subjective experience was different, the meaning of those receptions, interactions, and rites of passage were different as well. Thus, it paid to be a person of stature for one brother, AND it also paid to live off the grid for the other brother.

What survival mechanisms did you pick up along the way as compared with others in your family?

Being the class clown is one survival mechanism. Being the social butterfly is also a survival mechanism. Shyness, compulsivity, hesitance, and gregariousness are all traits we use

---

[18] Watkins, C. Edward. Birth-order research and Adler's theory: A critical review., Individual Psychology: Journal of Adlerian Theory, Research & Practice, Vol 48(3), Sep 1992, 357-368.

to get by—our "shtick," if you will. The class clown and social butterfly sit at packed lunch tables and are invited to parties. The introvert doesn't draw any undue attention to himself or herself and, in so doing, saves him- or herself from the perceived pain (or energy it takes) of speaking to others. Checking the locks or having your pregame ritual (however nonsensical it may be) makes you feel as if you've checked all the boxes—"you've done your homework." Being cautious keeps you from making mistakes and getting hurt. Or, so we all think!

The class president AND the nerd, with his face fixed on the computer screen, are both experiencing their own subjective truth. Maybe you consciously chose specific traits over others, based on your respective situation. Maybe you just figured, "This is how I am" (based on genetics, upbringing, experiences, etc.). In either case, the brain is doing its job to help you survive. Remember, we're a long way from foraging for food and sleeping with one eye open. Or are we? From an ego standpoint, social life and death still rely on some very primal wiring. For some, the class clown persona emerges because the thought of being disliked is too painful or invalidating. For others, the introvert persona emerges because the thought of all that attention is too painful or too much validation.

Survival is the avoidance of perceived pain—emotional, physical, or psychological—and the way we avoid exists on a continuum. Athlete A does everything she possibly can in her preparations, so she can check every proverbial box. This gives her room for some degree of comfort IF she doesn't win. Conversely, Athlete B feels just as much pain IF he loses. However, he takes a more casual approach in his preparations, doing only the minimum required training and relying on "natural talent." For him, the pain would be too great if he were to go the extra mile in his prep. The built-in excuse of what he "could" have done had he actually trained more is better for his ego.

But Athlete A is not off the hook either. What is it about her make-up that doesn't allow for just a little bit of fun? How does she know she's doing everything she can? Maybe everything includes doing nothing sometimes. Both athletes are concerned about two results: 1) How they do in competition and 2) how they are doing with competition. The first concern is about placement and standing once the game is over. "I got first," or "I qualified for the finals." The second concern has to do with the athletes' subjective well-being. "Boy, I feel nervous," or "Gee, I hope I'm ready." The more we believe, the more we see(k) evidence to back up our belief. This is how the lie becomes your truth. Incidentally, I am certain you may be thinking Athlete A's approach is better. It may very well be. But the brightest flame doesn't always burn the longest. Both flames however, do shine.

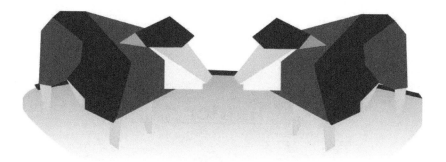

Revisiting the story of the two brothers . . . you may have been left asking: Which became CEO, and which became the artist?

Chapter 5

The CEO

"At every point in human existence someone somewhere decided to take that bite of cake. If you don't eat your cake, simply for the sake of keeping it whole, all you'll end up with is stale cake."

There is a large factory located somewhere between the 5 and 405 freeway in a part of Southern California that is not regularly frequented by tourists. There are offices in the front of the building, with a large warehouse in the back. Automated and manually operated machines occupy the warehouse.

Because the factory runs twenty-four hours a day, the front offices are not always accessible to employees working in the warehouse. There's a warehouse floor manager making sure time cards are punched, breaks are taken, and production schedules are met. The manager also has the responsibility of reporting issues on a given shift to the front office and/or CEO, not least of which is any incident involving safety standards. Most of the twenty-four-hour day is devoted to manufacturing and selling one product that comes in one size but several different colors. Business, albeit a bit mundane, is good. For as much machinery and personnel as this factory has, things run smoothly, and other than the natural social cliques that form at any workplace (with the ensuing psychodrama), employees rarely complain.

There was too much disruption when minor changes were attempted in the past, so it became somewhat of a corporate habit to maintain the status quo. Collectively, there was a sense of comfort on everyone's part due to perceived certainty. Middle management would raise concerns from time to time; the CEO would often agree, but in the end, the front office crew would always talk themselves out of making changes in an effort to keep things running smoothly. It was easy to justify not making changes that an outsider might find necessary because the factory was getting by just fine. Moreover, getting the unionized warehouse workers on board with any change, large or small, was a painful process.

However, the CEO himself was concerned on a daily basis. Thoughts swimming through his head: "The processes that worked so well in the past now seem to hinder the factory's progress. All of the machinery was paid off years ago, but maintenance costs are starting to eclipse procurement of a new system. The systems that allowed us to thrive now only allow us to survive. If new systems were to be put in place, retraining, hiring, firing, and dealing with loss of production during the transition would all be added costs. It could take up to a year before we're able to run smoothly again. I don't know if I have what it takes to handle such an undertaking."

Yet, he pressed forward on making the changes that were flashing red in his daily view of the business. As the last of the outdated equipment was being removed, the CEO said to himself: "What am I thinking!? Did I make the right decision? What if the new equipment doesn't fit? Or doesn't work? What if my projections are wrong? How will the employees adjust? Can I handle this change at my age?" Nonetheless, checks had been written, lines of credit had been established, and everyone in the front offices knew that if the factory was to compete, the best choice was to evolve.

The CEO woke up early to meet the trucks on the first day and watched closely as things were brought in and moved around and the retraining of his employees began. Several months later, the CEO, who was once on the floor every day, was now only a silhouette seen through the window of his office.

Business was running smoothly, and the factory was once again thriving. History repeated. His story repeated.

But how did this REALLY happen?

The truth is the simple version. The facts are not that easy: Everybody experienced some amount of "pain" during the transition. Workflow and profits were both interrupted for a time. New employees were hired, and existing employees were retrained, which meant many long-standing social connections were strained due to the new logistics. Floor workers learned and implemented new processes while front office staff created new stock keeping units (SKUs) and managed the increased scheduling, production, and personnel demands. By the ninth month, the factory was only at 80 percent automation, and there were more union meetings than normal during that time. Permits, lawsuits, and personal/family matters, ate away at initial gains made by the new efficiencies, and even though payroll (with raises) was being met, the real gains were not realized until years after the changes had been completed.

Our brains are much like the CEO and the factory in the story. Take a look at the next graphic:

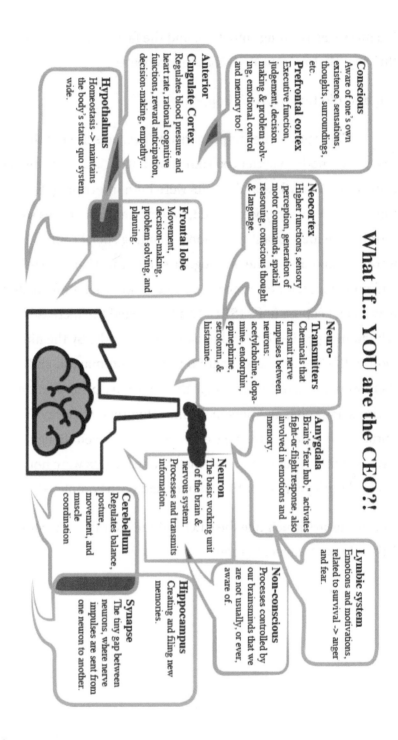

What If... YOU are the CEO?!

Now, let's look at the CEO story again. However, this time . . .

...You're the CEO!

There is a large factory (brain) located somewhere between the 5 and 405 freeway in a part of Southern California not regularly featured in movies. There are offices in the front (frontal lobe) of the building with large warehouse space (neocortex) in the back. Automated (subconscious) and manually operated machines occupy the warehouse space. Because the factory runs twenty-four hours a day (subconscious), the front offices (conscious) are not always accessible to employees working in the warehouse. There is a warehouse floor manager (anterior cingulate cortex) making sure time cards are punched, breaks are taken, and productions schedules are met. The manager (anterior cingulate cortex) also has the responsibility of reporting issues to the front office and/or CEO (prefrontal cortex); not least of which is making sure safety (amygdala) standards are met. Most of the twenty-four-hour day is devoted to manufacturing and selling only one product (survival) that comes in one package (you) but several different colors (you at work, at play, and in life). Business, albeit a bit mundane (homeostasis), is good. For as much machinery and personnel (all of your brain's parts and functions) as this factory has, things generally run smoothly. Other than the natural social cliques (synapses—neurons that fire together, wire together[19]) that form at any work place (neural pathways), employees don't complain.

It became habit to maintain the status quo, as there was too much disruption (in the amygdala) when minor changes were attempted in the past. Collectively (conscious and subconscious), there was a sense of comfort on everyone's part due to perceived certainty. Mid-level management (hypothalamus) would raise concerns from time to time; the CEO (prefrontal cortex) would often agree. In the end though, recertifying after major changes to meet OSHA[20] standards (amygdala) seemed too daunting, and they would always talk themselves out of making changes in an effort to keep things running at status quo. It was easy justifying not making any changes because the factory was getting by just fine. Moreover, getting the unionized warehouse floor workers (subconscious) on board with any change, large or small, was a painful process.

However, the CEO himself is concerned on a daily basis (hypothalamic-pituitary-adrenal axis[21]): The processes that

---

[19] Hebbian Theory—learning links neurons in new ways. When two neurons fire at the same time repeatedly (or when one fires, causing the other to fire) chemical changes occur in both, so that the two tend to connect more strongly.

[20] Occupational Health & Safety Administration. https://www.osha.gov/law-regs.html
[21] Randall, Michael. *The Physiology of Stress: Cortisol and the Hypothalamic-Pituitary-Adrenal Axis*, Dartmouth Undergraduate Journal of Science. http://dujs.dartmouth.edu/fall-2010/the-physiology-of-stress-cortisol-and-the-hypothalamic-pituitary-adrenal-axis#.VPf4tkK6d9g

worked so well in the past (BS) now seem to hinder the factory's progress. All of the machinery (subconscious) was paid off years ago, but maintenance costs are starting to eclipse procurement of a new system. What allowed the factory to thrive in the past (beliefs) now only allows it to survive. New systems mean retraining and hiring (adopting new beliefs), firing (letting go of limiting beliefs), and dealing with loss of production during the transition. Calculating how long the transition could take is insignificant to the importance of continued and focused growth.

As the last of the outdated equipment (old beliefs) was being removed, the CEO was saying to himself (Automatic Negative Thoughts[22]): "What am I thinking!? Did I make the right decision? What if the new stuff doesn't fit? Or doesn't work? What if my projections were wrong? How will the employees adjust? Can I handle this change at my age?" Nonetheless, checks had been written, lines of credit had been taken, and everyone in the front offices (prefrontal cortex/conscious) knew the factory had to evolve to succeed.

The CEO woke up early to meet the trucks on the first day. He worried (amygdala) as he closely watched things being brought in and moved around. As with most things in life, worries about "the thing" are worse than the actual thing itself.

---

[22] Beck Institute for Cognitive Behavior Therapy.
http://www.beckinstitute.org/history-of-cbt/

For several months the CEO (prefrontal cortex), accompanied by front office staff (conscious) ventured down to monitor warehouse activity. As time went on, warehouse floor workers (subconscious) saw less and less of the front office staff (new beliefs becoming the predominant neural pathways). The CEO who once was on the floor everyday was now only a silhouette seen through the window into his office. Business was running smoothly, and the factory was once again thriving.

But neurologically, how did this happen?

The truth is the simple version: repetition becomes habit. The facts are a bit more complex. Our subconscious and amygdala are the reasons we talk ourselves out of change. Everybody experiences growing pains. Adopting new behavior and breaking old habits takes hard effort and many of us do not like change. Workflow is disrupted; and profits may be delayed. The practice of careful investment and delayed gratification means we won't see profits initially. New employees are carefully hired while existing employees are retrained, which means many social connections (limbic system) have been strained due to the new order.

Floor workers learned and implemented new processes (belief systems), while front office staff (prefrontal cortex) created new stock keeping units (SKUs) and managed the increased scheduling/production demands.

By the ninth month, the factory was 80 percent fully

automated. Regularly scheduled meetings took place smoothly as if there were no new changes implemented just months prior. It was only when the front office staff (prefrontal cortex) compared the growth side by side that one could see the drastic changes from what once was to what exists now—a thriving and mentally fit organization!

The world, the factory, a family, and your own body are all ecosystems fighting to maintain homeostasis. The central issue with the CEO/factory story, as it pertains to your life and what you want, is that you know you can take advantage of this phenomenon rather than just exist within it. You have a choice. If you upset the balance enough, the fight for homeostasis will still rage. However, the settling point will not be the same as it was before you shook things up. Think of a fist pushing through a plastic bag. The bag stretches and stretches as pressure is consistently applied. When you take your fist out, the bag will retract, but it will never go back to its original state. It will, however, be able to accommodate more with good utility for some time. Ultimately, the bag does have a limit and will break if continuous pressure is applied. The punctured bag will clearly not hold much nor will it have the same utility as it once did. What was once a holding cell is now a conduit: a pass-through that is pliable, adaptable, and now open to new things, some of which can travel to and fro in either direction. In many ways, the bag with the hole in it allows us to grab other things that can teach us and help us to grow.

Chapter 6

Self-Esteem Is Not Enough—But You Are!

"What gets us into trouble is our inability to incorporate another system—failure to evolve in a world built to evolve."

It's almost as if we're trained to think we need to deal with adversity. But what if we are already preprogrammed to handle adversity? When "the going gets tough," especially with something we care about, we become aggravated or distracted, or we shut down. Yet if you think of a baby learning to walk, it's fair to say the infant didn't just get right up and start walking. Toddlers fall and keep adjusting. Those little champions somehow figure it out.

The "somehow" is the natural process of 100 billion unconnected neurons creating connections[23]; the "somehow" is our preprogrammed way of dealing with adversity. We all fall. Just know that when you fall, you fall forward.

Where the training lacks, especially among younger high performers, is in teaching how to deal with success. Intellectually, we don't always know—but we generally understand—that getting it right the first time is unlikely. On the way to getting it right, the journey or challenge may be difficult, and it surely won't feel right at times. Not everyone is accepted into Harvard. There are dots to be connected, such as graduating from high school with a certain grade point average or receiving an SAT score above 2100. Similarly, there is a process for becoming president, a CEO, or an Olympic medalist. Incidentally, none of those things are predetermined at birth; however, once you're there, what's it like? What do you do once you have everything you thought you wanted? More importantly, what if you reach a pinnacle at a very young age? What if you are a national champion at the age of twelve, financially able to retire before you're thirty-five, or win a Grammy when you're seventeen?

The reason so many actors, musicians, and top athletes struggle mentally and emotionally before the age of forty is due

---

[23] J. P. Shonkoff and D. A. Phillips, eds., *From Neurons to Neighborhoods: The Science of Early Childhood Development* (National Academies Press, 2000), http://www.nap.edu/catalog/9824.html;
R. Shore, *Rethinking the Brain: New Insights into Early Development* (New York, NY: Families and Work Institute, 1997), pp. 16–17.

to the incongruences of their subjective realities. It's a coveted position to be a child prodigy, but, as an adult, you're just someone who used to be a child prodigy. Many of the celebrated children who performed like adults gradually found themselves left wanting when, as an adult, they discovered their distinguishing characteristic was mitigated by the fact that others can match or eclipse their level of talent in the grown-up world. Being young and supremely talented affords large rewards. Unfortunately, the rewards aren't the same and quite often talents aren't the same when prodigies transition to adulthood or out of their initial field of expertise, whether it is in music, acting, sports, or other areas.

Child stars are given access to a world in which they must play the part, and this is after filming has ended for the day. Normal developmental milestones have been hurried, stifled, or skipped entirely. These children spend the beginning of their lives being told how great they are just for doing what they do, being who they are. Then some of them spend early adulthood not being told how great they are for doing what they do or being who they... were.

Those who successfully transition from one stage of life to the next are aware of potential, both internally ("I am now more capable of X") and externally ("My contributions can be impactful on or for Y"). Child stars who successfully transition to adult success recognize the work ethic challenges as they age and might actually take a break to be kids and, later, adults. Nurturing the thing they did naturally takes an internal drive on the adult playground for two reasons, as stated earlier: 1) The rewards are no longer the same externally, and 2) the rewards are no longer the same internally. Catchphrases or punch lines such as "What'chu talkin' bout, Willis?"[24] can lose their luster over time. The audience refines its comedic tastes, and there are newer, better, shinier, and more relevant jokes being told. Also, those delivering the joke may not get as much out of delivering the same punch line, as they too may have outgrown the old material.

Actors and comedians are not the only ones forced to transition into another stage of life. Many aging athletes find themselves wondering why the "big win" didn't feel as big as it used to feel. CEOs, accountants, lawyers, and doctors also face the same fate . . . eventually. They all soon learn that investing for retirement is more than just placing a percentage of income in a 401K or an IRA.

Year after year, the BMX World Championships was an event I would only read about in magazines. Seeing the guys I normally competed against—one year in Australia, another year in Holland—I had beaten them all at one time or another. Given the chance, I believed I could win that race.

My belief actually became a reality in short order—I was the winner of my first World Championship final! It took me by surprise and, at the time, I didn't know how I did

---

[24] The 1980s TV show, *Diff'rent Strokes*, often showed main character Arnold, played by Gary Coleman, saying this famous catchphrase. Coleman is also a great example of the proverbial child star.

it. During my most competitive years, it became my thing to chase after what seemed an elusive goal. When I became a father, it was my dream to stand on top of the podium as a champion with my infant son in my arms. Several years in a row proved to be good runs, and yet still no gold. Truth be told, my son was not able to attend those races anyway. No second world title. No photo op.

Thirteen years later, I found myself at the Pan American Games. The original belief was still the same: given the chance, I could win. This time, though, I knew how to win.

Some things you should know before we go further: I barely got the call to go. I was also the oldest competitor. I was back in school and knee-deep in my studies *and* had two papers due upon my return from Brazil.[25] Oh, and I was also a long shot to win, according to the press.

I won that race, by the way. The only lap I won all day was the final. Aside from the celebratory finish line antics, there was no son, no family, and only a few people I would call "friends" in attendance. My wife arranged a welcome party at the airport for my return. My son was too young to understand what was going on at the time, and all the noise in the terminal frightened him.

The last podium experience I had was not in Brazil, however. As my name was called to accept my diploma, I

---

[25] During that time, I reached out to the father of a young racer, as one of the papers I was writing was about high-performing young athletes. The father's name was Mike Fields. His son, Connor, won the PanAm Games four years later and went on to represent the USA at the 2012 Olympic Games in London.

saw my dad, mom, wife, and son, now the first of two, right there in the front row. On my way to the stage to officially become Doctor Jason Richardson, I made a small detour to give my son a kiss on the cheek. The little boy didn't know much about Daddy's days as an athlete, but he knew what a graduation was because he was a graduate of preschool. He also knew that this graduation meant Daddy became a doctor, and doctors help people.

For a guy who became a champion at the highest level, this small, obscure graduation proved my mettle more than the medals earned during my days racing. When I won as a young rookie, I didn't know how I did it. When I won as a seasoned veteran, I knew exactly how it was done. When I received my doctorate in front of the most important people in my world, I earned the elusive championship moment I had searched for on the track.

Having high self-esteem *does not* guarantee great results. There are plenty of incarcerated felons with an inflated self-view. Meanwhile, extremely successful people are known to grapple with a more moderate self-concept.[26] Self-esteem, while highly regarded and often warranted, is not necessary to produce achievement. *You*, however, *are* necessary to produce achievement!

---

[26] Ervin Staub. (1986). A conception of the determinants and development of altruism and aggression: motives, the self, and the environment. In: Carolyn Zahn-Waxler et al. (eds.) *Altruism and Aggression*. pp. 135-164. [Online]. Cambridge Studies in Social and Emotional Development. Cambridge: Cambridge University Press. Available from: Cambridge Books Online <http://dx.doi.org/10.1017/CBO9780511752834.007> [Accessed 06 April 2015].

Characteristics that are detrimental to an individual and society as a whole include high self-esteem coupled with no appreciable skills or individuals' beliefs that they can't truly accomplish anything. If you wonder how this is developed, just drop in on any organized youth ball game. Some "recreational" leagues will stop keeping score if the point spread becomes too big. In other leagues, no score is kept, and everyone is given a trophy.

Or how about modern birthday parties? A child is invited to another person's home to celebrate someone else's life yet becomes upset because there weren't any party favors. In a society where everyone receives a trophy, a rude awakening indeed comes when some kids later realize that some of those trophies were not actually earned. Once these kids reach the marketplace as young adults, the slap in the face is more profound if all they rely on is how good they feel about themselves versus what value they can provide.

Just being there definitely isn't enough in high-stakes competition. Just being there isn't enough at most places of employment. At least people acknowledge your presence in professional sports, but I'm not so certain there are fans lined up when you arrive for your first day at Cubicles-R-Us. Regardless of your job description or your station on the work, play, and life continuum, it's all high stakes. What do you bring to the table? What's your contribution? Just being there is easy. Showing up requires having "skin in the game."

The sleight of hand we want to watch for is when self-esteem replaces self-efficacy. Esteem places emphasis on how one is feeling; efficacy places emphasis on *what* one is capable of doing. Both high self-esteem and high self-efficacy are encouraged, but if pushed to choose, bet on efficacy every time. Thinking you can and believing you are able is a much better formula for success than just feeling good about oneself. In many cases, it may not feel good to do good; this is where the leaders separate themselves from the rest of the pack. In a family, it is the parents who keep their children at home when all the "other kids" are going to the party. In athletics, it's the veteran who knows when his time is up rather than continuing to suit up. In business, it's the person who has the heart to tell a partner or coworker the truth rather than what they want to hear.

In dealing with success and failure, the meaning we attach to both is more important than actually failing or succeeding and the frequency of those occurrences.[27] This is why earned success is important. Those earned outcomes help us derive meaning out of what we do, why we do it, and what we get out of it; however, letting outcomes define who you are detracts from the richness of your experiences. For instance, one can lose and not be a loser. One can be victimized and not be a victim. In work, play, and life, there is a "you're only as good as your last deal/finish/test" mentality as things become competitive. Sadly, this B.S. may have begun as a motivator but

---

[27] Martin V. Covington, "Making the Grade: A Self-Worth Perspective on Motivation and School Reform."

ultimately disenfranchises us from our potential because it becomes too much about the result and not enough about the task at hand.

Carol Dweck, author of *Mindset: The New Psychology of Success*, reminds us to focus on the effort. Place value in the work and personal gains made as you move forward. Think of yourself as continually developing or becoming. Feeling good (self-esteem) and doing good (self-efficacy) do not always coincide. Championship moments begin before you accept the check or stand on the podium. I hope those moments extend well beyond you stepping off the stage and cashing your last check. Remember, you are the baby who learned to walk despite the many failed attempts. *You* are enough, my friend. The question you need to answer is, "Do you believe you're enough despite how you feel at this very moment?"

peace of mind

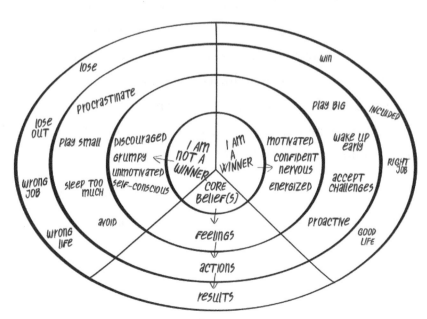

Chapter 7

This is some B.S.! Belief Systems

"In the game of life, anybody can win; but not everyone is a winner or believes they are!"

We all have formulated explanations about how and why we are the way we are. Genetics play a major role in what we are, while who we are is more a case of what we think we know about our family's origin sprinkled with amalgamations of recalled experiences. Nonetheless, your brain was wired through, with, and by nature and experience[28], even if we are poor curators of our own history.

---

[28] Chaney, Warren, *Workbook for a Dynamic Mind*, 2006, Las Vegas, Houghton-Brace Publishing, p. 44

Remember the brothers in Chapter 4? They essentially shared the same experiences and the same genetics. They had the same parents and even shared the same room; however, they looked at the world and themselves through individual lenses. More specifically, owing to the slightest differences in contextual placement (time/date of birth, height, skin tone, hair color, etc.), the world received them differently, and they each received a different world. Thus, the two brothers had vastly different vantage points, much like our friends watching the big game in Chapter 3. Your experience of what it's like to live in your body and the world contributes to the development and maintenance of your core beliefs. Some experiences may be more poignant, while other experiences are seemingly benign. Suffice it to say, each one of us has a set of beliefs. Those beliefs bring about feelings; feelings lead to actions, and the actions ultimately lead to results.

Straight B.S.!

Michael Jordan was arguably the best player in the history of basketball, but was it simply because he was just better than everyone else? When someone dominates in any given space, it's common for competitors to think the dominating person is somehow more gifted or even *destined* for such preeminence: "My goodness, he's a machine!" Jordan's case is legendary. Any fan of the game can regale you with an anecdote about MJ's ability to work harder or jump higher than everyone else. People, including the other players, believed he was "that much better." Which is exactly the point—the others *believed* it.

If you are playing a game and you believe the other person is better, more gifted, talented, perhaps even anointed, your brain will have already worked out why you lost to that person. It could even rationalize why it was okay that you lost despite the fact that you really wanted to win. In other words, the validation of your belief that "the other guy is better" trumps your own desire to win. Ouch! It happens everywhere: in the boardroom, on the track, on the little league field. Because being right, at least subconsciously, is more important than beating the best.

No basketball player likes getting dunked on, or, worse yet, stuffed while taking a shot. But what if the shortest guy in the league does it? What if that same guy swats the ball away as you take your next shot? If a Jordan type dunks on a guy or a LeBron type denies your shot, it still hurts, but it's easier to take because "he's the best." It is one thing to have some player who normally rides the bench challenge your beliefs, but it is quite another to have the highest paid guy in the league confirm them.

Consider race, gender, class, money, and food. If you want to discover a person's beliefs, bring any of these subjects up in conversation: "Taller guys win elections, blondes are invited to more parties, and black males get to ride in elevators by themselves more often. . . generally." These are not the most politically correct statements, but they likely struck a nerve when you read them. The first two can actually be statistically proven, while the third is based on anecdotal evidence from my conversations with other black males. All three examples, however, should resonate on a deeper level because they are tied to stereotypes. "Widely held, but fixed and oversimplified images or ideas about a particular type of person or thing";[29] all these sound suspiciously like beliefs. Looking at the regularity of stereotypes can make you wonder how they are so easily developed. Dr. Rob Irwin, fellow sport and performance psychologist, explains this (and any other belief) with the concept and use of the Belief Matrix.

Dr. Irwin would be the first to tell you he wasn't an "early riser." If you went to one of his training sessions, you would hear that he grew up thinking he had the "bad gene" because everyone else in his family seemed to be able to achieve good grades and get along. He barely escaped military school by graduating with a B- average.

It wasn't until he realized that his bad gene theory was BS, that he hit his stride academically and professionally and on the golf course. Fortunately for you (and me), he was able to reengineer his successes and share with us how this happens and begins in the brain.

29

http://www.oxforddictionaries.com/us/definition/american_english/stereotype

Reengineering Belief with Dr. Rob Irwin, Ph.D.

Most everything (your job, your home, your clothes, your friends, etc.) is based on your beliefs. Ninety percent of the total scientific knowledge about the brain has been discovered in just the last fifteen years. Neurologists, social scientists, and thought leaders, such as Richard Restak, M.D.; Louis Cozolino; and Rick Hanson, Ph.D. are changing the way we think about (our) thinking[30]—more importantly, how our brains/minds connect and work. As long as we continue to think, our brains can grow.

The pathways and connections work much like our road system in the United States. Sometimes we see a better way, but until the road is built, we are forced to take the scenic route. In many cases, we are so used to traveling a certain way that we don't know or see alternative routes. For example, the CEO and his factory workers were dealing with a bit of both. So either we are entrenched in our beliefs and do not see another way, or we see the other way but our beliefs do not let us blaze the new trail. Why? Because your thinking brain (conscious brain), the part actively figuring out what you want for dinner as you drive home, does not have the same capability as your nonconscious brain, the part that automatically gets you home without any

---

[30]http://youtu.be/jpuDyGgIeh0, http://www.amazon.com/The-Neuroscience-Psychotherapy-Interpersonal-Neurobiology/dp/0393706427, http://www.thegreatcourses.com/professors/richard-restak/.

thinking.[31] This nonconscious part picks up millions of bits of information every second of every day of your life, the things that go into your brain, of which you are unaware.[32] Whereas the thinking brain, the portion aware of things entering your mind, works serially as in the case of learning a dance routine or writing down directions to make a sandwich. If you were to do either for the first time, you might find the process painfully slow or just plain painful! However, once you get past the pain of learning the routine, the process can become automatic, maybe even enjoyable. The bottom line: your nonconscious brain is far faster than your conscious brain. It's the difference between sending or receiving messages via horse and buggy versus text messaging!

The speed and efficiency of your nonconscious brain are precisely the reason it is so difficult to get yourself out of a rut. Visualize actual ruts on a slope or mountain. They were formed because it was the most efficient way for water to flow down the hill. It would take great effort to reroute the water. However, once rerouted, the water will eventually create a new preferred path of least resistance based on the initial effort. If the new path is not cut deep enough or used enough, the water will flow down the original paths. The reason it is difficult for us get out of a rut is due to the (brain's) desire for comfort, familiarity, or safety. Just like the water flowing down a hill, the information

---

[31] There is thinking . . . it's just so fast and automatic that we are unaware of these processes most of the time.
[32] http://psychlopedia.wikispaces.com/nonconscious+processes

that flows through our brains travels the paths of least resistance unless we impose a new demand.

Technology enables us to photograph images 1/100,000 the size of a human hair, which allows us to see that our brains are not limited to a fixed number of cells but rather have the ability to grow on an almost unlimited scale. For example, neurologists can take a picture of your brain in January. If you then decide to speak differently, think differently, or do things differently, such as immersing yourself in language lessons, and you return for another brain picture in June, you will see visible, living evidence of growth. Learning a new skill, as hard as it may have been, created a new connection. When a connection is created and those same areas of the brain keep firing together, they ultimately *wire* together.[33] Practicing things frequently leads to automation. Things performed automatically and frequently lead to mastery. Mastery on demand leads to instinct.

What usually causes major changes in beliefs for most people are life-changing events: some form of trauma, some form of fortune, this book, and so on. But what if we could take advantage of what we know about our brain? What if we could proactively program or train our brains?

---

[33] Hebb, D.O. (1949). *The Organization of Behavior*. New York: Wiley & Sons.

Athletes in a rut or slump will often lament about how they "are thinking too much out there." On some deeper level, they recognize that conscious thinking is getting in the way of what they know they can do. People perform best when they perform automatically. What if you automatically shut down when it's time to perform? This is the parlor trick everyone comes to Mindstudio for[34]. "How can I trick myself into not caring?" "I just want to turn my brain off, Doc!" "How come I do it perfectly all day and then choke in the final?" Their brains are performing automatically, and in each one of those instances, their brains are cluing in to something of which they are not yet aware. Being angry with yourself for caring about something you really do care about will definitely send "discomfort" signals to your brain. Trying to turn your brain off in the heat of the moment will send "unfamiliar" signals to your brain. "Kicking butt" all day in qualifying rounds, only to find yourself waiting for something to go wrong in the final? Yep, your brain's thinking this is pretty "unsafe."

Athletes are not alone. How many of us tense up when the boss drops in? Could you perform your best skill for 10 million dollars on TV with a live audience *and* 10 million viewers? You only get one shot, by the way. Actually, I think you *could* succeed, but I'm uncertain if you *would*. I am certain the feeling and execution, even if successful, would not be the same

---

[34] What we call the office space Dr. Irwin and I Share.

as in your home when no one is watching and nothing's on the line.

One of the reasons we underperform may be due to a lack of skills that enable us to calm down or talk to ourselves in ways that trigger those moments we want or had when performing well. I argue that it is also the lack of use of those skills, as many are unaware they possess such abilities. The other reason we underperform is due to our programming. Anything that registers in our brains as uncomfortable, dangerous, or unfamiliar renders us more susceptible to undesirable performance.

We have approximately 70,000 thoughts per day.[35] And because most everyone agrees we are creatures of habit, we can safely say that most of the thoughts we have—even if we are unaware—are the same thoughts we had the previous day. This is a good thing, by the way. Otherwise, we would have to learn to walk and brush our teeth again each new day. We are supposedly at the top of the food chain because of our ability to reason and exercise a small thing called free will.

Remember, your conscious (thinking brain) works more slowly, *but* you can actively control what information goes in. Your nonconscious brain works faster than your Wi-Fi connection, and it works automatically (without case-sensitive

---

[35] Laboratory of Neuroimaging
http://www.loni.usc.edu/about_loni/education/brain_trivia.php

passwords). When you learn something, you consciously enter the data into your hard drive and keep entering data until the program runs itself. It's rare we forget how to ride a bike once we learn. What does this mean for you? Your conscious brain trains your nonconscious brain. Also, your nonconscious brain keeps those learned habits from being forgotten.

As best we can, it is our responsibility to proactively train the thoughts and behaviors we want in order to attain the results we desire. The caveat is that the brain is always working for us, which means it is sometimes working against us. This means anything deemed new or difficult may be red-flagged by our nonconscious brains. Unions sometimes threaten to strike when they encounter demands they don't like, right? You may want to ride a snowboard like Shaun White, but your brain may have another opinion when you consider hitting the rail or dropping in on the half pipe. As the CEOs of our lives, it is incumbent upon us to work *with* our resources rather than work against them. Power is always preferred to force.[36]

Enter The Matrix—with Dr. Rob Irwin, Ph.D.

The chain of events: Beliefs → Feelings (Emotion) → Actions → Results. Beliefs drive feelings. Feelings drive actions. Actions drive results.

---

[36] http://www.amazon.com/Power-Force-David-Hawkins-Ph-D/dp/1401945074

Example (It's a bit oversimplified, but you'll get the picture):

Belief →	Feelings →	Actions →	Results!
I can win/I come through for people.	Motivated, anxious (as opposed to stressed), focused, inspired	Wake up early, accept challenges, act proactively, play big, play to your strengths	Win, place, or show. High conversion rates.
I don't belong/ I'm not ready	Fearful, stressed, angry, unmotivated, reactive	Poor follow-through, avoid challenges, waste time on Facebook rather than engaging in tasks	Did not qualify. No Sale. Low conversion rates.

Important note: We are very good at keeping our beliefs in "silos." This compartmentalization allows us to have competing beliefs, both within a given subject and among different subjects. Think of the athlete who does well in a certain city or venue but struggles at others. Or think of yourself with your friends versus with your parents. Do you talk differently with your friends? Do you act differently with your parents? Both groups represent two different systems, and it is *very* possible or likely that you hold different beliefs in each system.

Here's another important note: Not every bad result is your fault. You can believe in your ability and still not get the job or win the title fight. Other people cheat. Others may have a stronger belief. You may have a bigger belief such as "I'm unlucky" that interferes with your "I can win" belief, or maybe you were sick that day. Stranger things have happened.

That said; if you are willing to take accountability anyway, AND you are tired of the results you are earning, why not find out what's going on inside your head (heart and mind)? The Belief Matrix is a powerful tool to help you uncover a belief that holds you back. Every tool comes with a warning label. This one is no different:

1. It is highly recommended that you use this tool with a coach, trainer, mentor, or close friend or family member, as it is easier for them to see what you are projecting while you are busy protecting (your ego).

2. When working the matrix, put your worst foot forward. You'll know when the mirror shows an accurate reflection.

Time to "flip the script!" Feel free to fill in the blanks in the graphic below. You may want to use a pencil.

Start:

Lane 8). Write down an outcome (result) in your work, play, or life that you didn't want or don't like.

Lane 7). List the actions, YOUR ACTIONS, which may have led to the result you wrote down in lane 8.

Lane 6). This one is tricky! Write down the feelings and

emotions you had that could have driven the actions you just wrote down in lane 7. Be careful, once we get to lane 6, there can be overlap (crowding) with either the belief lane or the action lane. Work hard to distinguish between each lane for the sake of this exercise.

Lane 5). List thoughts (dare we say *beliefs*?) that would lead you to feel what you just wrote down in lane 6?

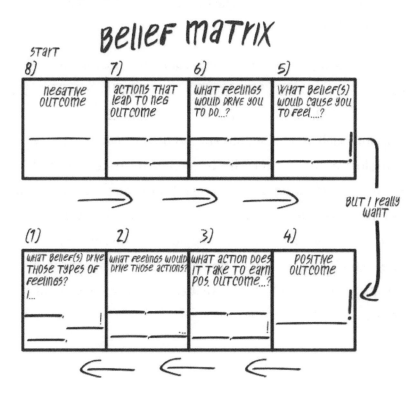

Now you're on the inside track...

Lane 4). State what (outcome) you want.

Lane 3). To get what you want, write down the actions you think it takes to make lane 4 work. (Remember the chain: Beliefs→Feelings→Actions→Results)

Lane 2). Tricky section again! You may feel crowded by lanes one and four. Focus! What emotions would give you the best shot in lane 3?

Lane 1). Pole position. List the thoughts or beliefs that would dominate lane 2.

The guarantee: It won't feel good to uncover a belief that holds you back. And admitting this is actually the case isn't any easier. Your blatant honesty about something that's not working, such as a belief, has started the formation of a new neurological connection. This is the time to strike. Stanford University's Huntington's Outreach Project states the following as it pertains to promoting brain reorganization, "Even simple brain exercises such as presenting oneself with challenging intellectual environments, interacting in social situations, or getting involved in physical activities will boost the general growth of connections."[37]

---

[37] http://web.stanford.edu/group/hopes/cgi-bin/wordpress/2010/06/neuroplasticity/#neuronal-growth-factors

<u>Chapter 8</u>

Will That Be Paper Or Plasticity?

"When you learn something, you consciously enter the data into your hard drive and keep entering data until the program runs itself. It's rare we forget how to ride a bike once we learn."

Until now, the client with the car, the brothers, the factory, the CEO, the guys watching the game, and the athletes with two distinct styles of preparation were all ways to convey different concepts. Now that the illustrations have been made, where do we hang the pictures that have been painted? What does this mean for you?

Your brain is constantly changing physically and functionally based on interaction with . . . well, everything. Plasticity, also known as neuroplasticity, is the brain's ability to rewire itself by rerouting information or processing functions to different areas or neural networks.[38] Learning, memory, and changes in abilities for which your brain is responsible illustrate how the concept of plasticity applies to all of us. [39]

As simple as the best things in life can be, life itself is more complex. We drive at high rates of speed on superhighways while texting, changing radio stations, rewrapping a child's burger to hand to him in the back seat, AND thinking about all the stuff that happened or all the stuff we "gotta do" when we arrive to wherever it is we are speeding. Yet we still fumble when giving directions to places we drive to every day. "What was the name of that street again? The one with the yellow house on the corner?"

So much is packed into our lives: the Google family calendar, work, homework, date nights, soccer, band practice, and more homework—and let's not forget somehow turning your passion in to a new career. Everyone is an entrepreneur these days. Apparently we're all becoming "brands" instead of

---

[38] Johnson, Joni E. *Psychology for Dummies* (not you, me!)
[39]Nubach, Daniel. *The Brain Explained*. There are two other areas: Brain development and brain damage. The former has to do with actual growth of brain matter and pruning of neurons and the latter deals with the brain finding new ways to communicate with itself to take advantage of remaining intact brain locations.

people. The more we pack in, the more we are impacted. All the while, our brains are sifting through interpreted data for the stuff that will allow us to get back home. Things with meaning generally get priority over everything else when it comes to the sifting. All of us have a complex system of *yes/no* and *if/then, else* decision trees that become lit up by triggers, known and unknown.

Our brains send information to certain places based on the connections we have, or the specific routing, often without us knowing how the information got there and often discarding superfluous information such as the names of streets to maintain efficiency. The whole time this information is being transmitted, your brain is still keeping you alive—heart beating, eyes blinking, and so on. We have become so efficient at being efficient that we don't even realize that the Fro-Yo on the corner closed two months ago.

Moving forward, the following is what you want to know about plasticity:

1. Because the brain adapts to its environment, it will adapt to a negative environment just as readily as it will to a positive one.
2. The extent of a brain's plasticity is dependent on the stage of development and the particular brain system or region affected.

Bruce Perry and Erin Hambrick say the following: "In fact, this brain plasticity is what allows us to keep learning into adulthood and throughout our lives."[40]

What gets us in trouble is our inability to incorporate another system. There is a reason this book is not being written on a typewriter and why you may be listening to this rather than reading it. Things evolve. Some of us, however, fail to evolve because we don't want to, we forget to, or we are scared of evolution itself. We are comfortable in some of our ruts.

Here are three questions you may want to ask yourself:

1. In which direction is my brain growing/changing/evolving?
2. In which direction do I want my brain to grow/change/evolve?
3. What can I do to promote adaptations that will allow me to thrive?

People don't go to bed weighing 175 lbs. with a full head of hair only to wake up the next morning fat and bald! It happens over time. Time passes regardless of whether or not we move forward. Plasticity is always in play. Let's use time to our advantage.

---

[40]Berry, Bruce P., and Hambrick, Erin P. *The Neurosequential Model of Therapeutics*
http://aia.berkeley.edu/strengthening_connections/handouts/perry/NMT_Article_08.pdf

Chapter 9

The Infinite Continuum: Been There, Done That!

"History repeated . . . His story—repeated!"

Our lives exist on an infinite continuum that precedes us and extends well beyond us. If we look closely at our existence in its totality, we may find that history repeats itself though the context has changed.

Professional BMX and Mountain Bike cyclist, Mike Day, offers his personal account just before he won Olympic Silver in Beijing. He also illustrates the relationship we all have with the *Infinite Continuum*:

Walking up to the start ramp for the Olympic final, so many crazy thoughts were buzzing around inside my head. I managed to stay focused, and I'm as ready as I'm ever going to be for the thirty-six seconds that come next. Then, "Hold up! Commercial break." WHAT?!

The commercial only lasts thirty seconds or so, but it feels like thirty minutes. More time to think. You spent the last four years thinking about this lap, and a thirty-second pause for a cereal commercial is all that stands in the way. It's unreal—maybe surreal.

When I started racing, I felt the same pressure at my local BMX track. Then I moved to state-level races, then to nationals. The pressure I felt before the Olympic final in Beijing was the same for me that it had been at every level of competition. Yes, I had problems dealing with it at times, but I found a few things that really helped me get ready for the task at hand.

-The first element that worked best for me was to make sure I did everything I could possibly do in training to get ready for the race.

-Second, treat every practice session as if it were the main event you are getting ready for; learn to practice at the same level you race.

-Third, the most important thing you can do is focus on what you can control. Don't waste energy on things that you cannot control.

Pressure is helpful to keep your race day focus razor-sharp. But when you stop to think about it, what is pressure really? It's something we create in our own heads. It's not something tangible, but it can still get in your way. Learn how to deal with it before it becomes overwhelming.[41]

—Mike Day – GT Bicycles, 2008 Olympic Silver Medalist, BMX Racing

---

[41] http://pedals2medals.com/winningwednesdays-back-issues-e-book/

Mike Day riding a fine line on the Continuum

Watch any classic western film, and you'll see a guy riding his horse for what is supposed to be miles and hours or days. The joke with these movies is that, if you look close enough, you'll see the horse and his rider pass the same rock or tumbleweed over and over again. Mike, in his account of what it felt like on the starting hill for the Olympic final, was clear when he said, "The pressure I felt before the Olympic final in Beijing was the same for me that it had been at every level of competition." Was there a glitch in the matrix as he was walking up the ramp?[42] How could it be that Mike saw the same tumbleweed blow by in Beijing, China, 2008 that he saw in Valencia, California, 1994?

Whether Olympian or weekend warrior, homebuilder or homemaker, executive or assistant, the same pressure exists at every level. It's our *perception* of the pressure that gets in the way or helps us along. It's the stress felt or applied that distracts or engages us. When Dr. Irwin helps us reengineer belief, the skill building is in the creation of new habits that allow for better automated responses. In theory and in practice, having gone through something makes it easier to go through it the next time. Because we do have a relationship with time, as well as the what, when, where, and why, it's important we slow down to go faster and farther. You have most likely "been there, done that" before. If we're not paying attention, we'll miss the rock or tumbleweed rolling by. And if we miss those subtle cues, how else are we to know that we've been there before? How else are we to know that we have already done that?

---

[42] "From the 1999 film *The Matrix*: Referring to a human experiencing déjà vu as caused by the machines altering the matrix."
http://www.urbandictionary.com/define.php?term=glitch+in+the+matrix

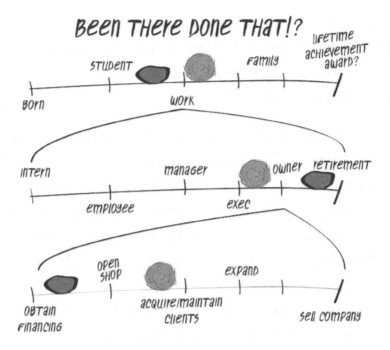

We often pass the same rock or tumbleweed during different stages of our lives

The *continuum* precedes us and extends beyond us. And while the context changes, like the jump from little league to big league or intern to middle manager to CEO, the fundamentals are the same—cycles within cycles. There's no doubt the star QB can translate his leadership instincts to the boardroom, even though he is a "rookie" businessman. Similarly, Mike was aware he felt the same nerves just before the Olympic final that he did in his first race when he was ten years old. Mike came through in that final, and he almost won because he was fully aware of his place and relationship within the continuum. And, though riddled with thoughts and emotion, he was exactly where he wanted to be. Life wasn't compartmentalized. He was nervous AND ready. Most importantly, he was in control enough to know when to let go and trust his instincts.

Chapter 10

Fighting Over the Emote Control: Feelings are Not Facts

"Thinking you can, believing you are able is a much better formula for success than just feeling good about oneself. In many cases, it may not feel good to do good; and, this is where the leaders separate themselves from the rest of the pack."

The biggest misconception in performance is thinking one has to *feel* a certain way to do a certain thing. Sure, how many people wouldn't like to feel their best and then actually do their best? This is an aspirational pursuit, and we would all be well served to have such an experience.

However, given what you now know about the brain, how it works, and the rules it sets to keep you alive or your ego protected are perfect conditions, or decent ones, necessary? Do you *have* to feel good to do good? Well, yes—*if* those are the rules you have set for yourself.

The "Mathlete"

Now, let's fast-forward to a session with a perfectly trained Olympic athlete in our studio. One of the hardest things to deal with for any top performer is the anxiety and frustration the athlete associates with underperforming. In many cases, it's not the lack of ability that debilitates athletes, but rather their fear, anxiety, and rigidity caused by being caught up in how they feel versus focusing on what they're supposed to do.

My brother-in-law is an accountant and is beyond good with numbers. I spent most of my early adult years living an athlete's existence, while he was clocking in to a nine-to-five every day. As we both transitioned deep into fatherhood, my house became the chosen place for the grandparents to watch all the children as we went off to do our hunting and gathering. My brother-in-law would wake up earlier than I did every day, drop off his kids, go to work, sometimes pick up one or both of his kids up, take his son to practice, and/or coach a team on weekends. He was, and still is, also kind enough to do our taxes "in his spare time."

One afternoon I called his office, expecting to leave a quick message on his voice mail if he didn't pick up, when an

unfamiliar voice answered, "Good afternoon. Mr. Williams' office!" At this point, I'm thinking to myself, "This guy has someone screening his calls? Really?!"

After I got off the phone, I sat and wondered, "Which one of us is really a high performer?" There are plenty of professionals with receptionists, but this was Ryan, the guy who drove the same car since college! I may have been the one with sponsors and magazine covers, but he was the one quietly (and consistently) stacking his chips.

Thinking of the story of my brother-in-law, I ask the same question, "Who is the high performer, you or the accountant?" I have posed this question to many elite athletes of every stripe, and the knee-jerk answer is overwhelmingly, me! (Of course, right?). Then I relay to them the part about him showing up every morning to drop off the kids; and at this point, I add that I really don't always know how he is feeling all the time. I don't know if his desk is ergonomically correct. I don't know what version of QuickBooks he uses. I don't hear him complain about his boss, workload, stress, changes in the tax code, and so on. Then, I ask again, "Who is the high performer?" Is the high performer the one saying, "I'm over it" because he didn't get the latest prototype product from one of his sponsors? Is the high performer the one with the luxury of deciding whether he is going to the gym at nine a.m. or eleven a.m.? Is the high performer the one refusing to show up because his teammate got the cover of the catalogue rather than him? Or is the high performer the guy who shows up every day and accounts for millions of dollars? The guy who pays someone else to screen *your* call! At this point, the pin drops, and everyone in the room can hear it!

In other words, the game (sport, life, business) doesn't care how you feel; showing up to play your best is what matters. Your family and friends care how you feel. So win, lose, or draw, you can count on being able to cry on their shoulders. They will comfort you, or try to at least. If you are looking for comfort as you enter the arena, you may have come to the wrong place. If you are looking for a shot to show your mettle, test your beliefs, or actually win, this is the place you want to be, and sometimes it serves us well to check our baggage at the curb in order to travel more freely.

The Power of "AND"

The dirty little secret about high performance is that (drum roll) it is not about skill building, but rather *instinct* building. Once you have honed your skills to the point of mastery, the only thing left in your way of evidencing your mastery is you. More specifically, there is a tendency to believe our emotional state has to be optimal, whatever that is, for us to do our best. Notice, I didn't say *be* at our best. We can do our best despite how we feel in the moment.

If you're nervous or scared, you may not like how you

feel. After all, who would? Think of your feelings as a cluster of gauges in an automobile. With gas prices fluctuating up and down, then back up again; most people probably have their eyes on the gas gauge. Add the fact that they might be late, the weather is foul, or that maybe it'll be three cents cheaper tomorrow, stopping to fill up becomes even more of a pain. Nonetheless, that light comes on once we get past a certain point on the gauge. If we only focus on our negative feelings about our gas tank running low, what happens? We run out of gas.

Many of us try to ignore the feelings we don't like. Anger, anxiety, sadness, fear—there are countless times a person has walked into the studio wanting to rid themselves of negative, albeit very natural, feelings. Paradoxically, trying to ignore the negative emotions only makes them grow from a distraction to THE distraction. Some feelings are easier to ignore than other feelings and you might even get away with it for a while. The gas gauge is urgent and something we want to take care of more immediately than a check engine light, depending on the type of car. However, those gauges are there for a reason, and if the engine light is ignored long enough, you may end up finding yourself stranded on the side of the freeway when you least expect it.

The cluster of human emotions works much like the gauges in our vehicles. Our emotions, good or bad, wanted or unwanted, positive or negative, are just telling us that something is important. They're saying to us, "This matters." Your emotions are there for a reason too. The reason it feels bad to lose is not to affirm some irrational belief that you suck or that they cheated! It's to remind you, by way of pain, to motivate yourself to go out there and do something about it next time! Complaining about getting gas will not fill up your tank. The feeling you get from sitting on the side of the road will keep you from running out again. Accepting your circumstances and taking the time to change them will always keep you running with enough in the tank.

Back to my accountant brother-in-law. The point is not that he doesn't have emotions. The guy is human, just like any one of us. I am sure there are times his wife is on his back and his kids are sick with the flu. Given his level in his profession, he too contends with the hazards of that very profession just like anyone else. The difference is that this guy doesn't say, "I'm over it" or "It is what it is." He does something about it. The reason he is so successful is directly correlated to his efficiency at keeping his eye on the ball, and he juggles many! The moral of the story is being responsible and mature. He is responsible to his feelings, not beholden to or stifled by them. And he is mature enough to accept them AND do his work anyway. Thus, his overall disposition is much healthier (and more profitable) than many so-called high performers.

Emotional control is the practice of accepting your emotions and doing the job anyway. Being on the line at the

Olympics is stressful enough. Pitching your ideas to a major account is stressful enough. Trying to explain to your wife why you need another flat screen TV, car, or power tool is harrowing enough! Why distract yourself with the task of avoiding or fighting something that is going to be there anyway? Your emotions and feelings are going to be with you, whether you want them there or not, until you actually deal with the situation.

Once you accept your emotional states as real, those emotions cease to be the facts. This means that you may *feel* bad but doesn't mean you *are* bad. Or the situation may be difficult, but that doesn't mean *you* have to be. Feeling nervous as you prepare for the Olympic final is an appropriate feeling, just as anger is an appropriate feeling when something is stolen from you. Both emotions may be considered negative because most people don't like to be nervous or angry. Yet both emotions carry with them just as much energy, and sometimes more, as do positive emotions. When we stop fighting ourselves, we are free to keep our eyes on the ball and allow the energy of our emotions to serve us in a positive way down the stretch.

A Quick Word on Positive and Negative

People don't have a problem seeing themselves in the car they want or picturing themselves cashing the big check. The disconnect is between the vision and the work it takes to get there. What does that look like? How do I do that? People get really stuck on how! The thing with the best-

selling self-help book, *"The Secret[43],"* as much as it's good hype and as much as people get charged up whether they read it or see the movie, is that it's just hype—superstition at best. The law of attraction will not work if you are not willing to do the work! Million-dollar thoughts require million-dollar actions. Championship thoughts require championship effort. You may or may not attract what you want, but you will definitely repel what you want if no real effort is made toward the things you want.

Just because you're thinking good thoughts, or positive thoughts, doesn't mean they're working positively for you. That puts a whole twist on the idea of positive and negative. The truth is there are many people who doubt. And you know, a lot of doubt has led to many great achievements. Most people would think doubt is negative. However, if you're walking on the street and someone punches you in the face, I'm guessing you're going to feel pretty upset, angry, hurt, or sad, and all those would be considered negative feelings. Those negative thoughts would cause a reaction such as, "I'm punching you back," calling the cops, or, "I'm going to run my fastest away from you because I'm in danger!" In each case, those negative emotions serve a positive purpose. When I'm working with athletes or whomever, I don't get too caught up in positive versus negative. I view those thoughts or those feelings as

[43] *The Secret* is a book based on the premise that "all you have to do is think about a thing and it will be so." It offers false hope to people and does a disservice to those really looking to make changes in their lives. It's empty optimism. Dream big, but be willing to do the work! Also, be ready to accept the consequences if it doesn't work out the way you dreamt it.

energy and train how we can harness that energy to serve us. The whole thing that *The Secret* is missing is the work! There's work involved, and by the way, just because a thought is negative and we don't like it doesn't mean it's not useful or can't serve a purpose. Are we going to dwell on the fact that we're feeling upset? Are we going to dwell on the fact that it's hard to win? Or that we're being bullied? Or are we going to do something about it? There are plenty of times people are not necessarily feeling good, but they show up anyway. It's the showing up and having the intention of "I want X" or the intention of "This is how I'm executing my plan" (even if it changes) that we actually start to see the benefits down the road.

It takes just as much responsibility to manage our wanted emotions as it does our unwanted emotions. Many competitors think confidence or excitement was all they needed. Yet, they came up short or didn't qualify for the final. They were left wondering, "What happened? I felt great." They looked the best in practice; doing the things no one else would even attempt. How could it be they were left watching rather than (still) participating?

Our emotions can be the distraction, even the ones we want. Rather than plainly accepting those positive emotions, some of us rely on them. Next thing you know, the fastest person at the race is slacking on the warm-up, a manager is not keeping track of time, and the genius garage start-up guy is possibly underestimating the competition. In other words, the athlete's, or executive's, or entrepreneur's eyes are off the ball. All of us are sometimes blinded by our own elation. The control is in the acceptance of the emotion, any emotion, as you stay on task.

It's An All-Inclusive Deal: The Magic Lamp

If a genie granted you a wish and guaranteed EVERYTHING you ever wanted in life as long as you worked for it, would you take that deal? What if a condition of the guarantee required that you contend with the same emotions that you would if no such guarantee wish were granted? Would that change things for you? Remember, you're guaranteed to get (earn) everything you've ever wanted.

When I present this scenario to clients, most take the deal, and some are disappointed that I'm not the genie! Somehow, the so-called negative emotions are acceptable when the outcome is guaranteed. So it's okay to suffer as long as you win? It's fine to feel nervous or scared as long as you know you'll come out smelling like roses? This far-fetched scenario positions our emotions as part of the process rather than as just a by-product of the process. There are no such guarantees, of course; but it does show our ability to come to terms with or reconcile our emotional state(s). From that standpoint, the genie scenario isn't so far-fetched. Ultimately, on the way to getting what we want, we may deal with some things we don't want. So ask yourself these two questions: "Is what I want worth how I feel right now?" and "Is what I want worth what I may go through on my way to getting it?" The bottom line is that you can win AND not feel your best! Isn't that a more competitive mindset than "I have to feel my best to win?"

Chapter 11

You Better Reconcile! Start Counting . . .

"If you are looking for comfort as you enter the arena, you may have come to the wrong place. If you are looking for a shot to show your mettle, test your belief, or actually win, this is the place you want to be, and sometimes it serves us well to check our baggage at the curb in order to travel more freely."

In financial terms, according to my accountant brother-in-law, reconciliation is the process of comparing transactions and activity to supporting documentation and resolving any discrepancies that may exist.[44] The process of reconciliation ensures the accuracy and validity of the information.[45]

---

[44] How fitting that Chapter 11 uses a financial metaphor. Coincidence or.... Destiny? Hopefully none of us are bankrupt of hopes and dreams—or the willingness to make them come to be.

[45] University of Washington, Finance & Facilities http://f2.washington.edu/fm/fa/internal-controls/reconciliation

The simplest way to avoid being eaten by a shark is to stay out of the water! The best way to avoid feeling nervous before a competition is to avoid competing. Okay, problem solved. Let's all go home! Wait? Oh . . . you like surfing? You like winning?! Then let's keep going.

If you like to surf, then you have come to accept the possibility of a shark attack. If you like winning in head-to-head competition, you have reconciled the fact that you may not like how you feel during the competition itself. If something is important enough on our to-do list, we *rationalize* very well. "The odds of a shark attack are . . ." or "I'm only nervous before I get on the start line . . ." Admittedly, this type of brain training is easier to do when it's something external we are working to justify. It becomes a much more hazardous journey when we are the ones placing the roadblocks in front of our own success.

This warrants more of a gut check. As the stakes rise, you will most likely feel as if you have more to lose. If it is not worth it, then don't do it. Your sanity does have value, *but recognize that the decision to jump ship early can come back to haunt you.* If, however, it is worth it, we are going to want to up the ante on that bet rather than play it safe.

The brain strives for harmony. The uneasiness caused by the chasm between your current place (physical or otherwise) and where you want to be is called *dissonance*. This lack of harmony will lead you to either lower your expectations or get to work to achieve what you want. Either way, things must match up in the brain to avoid malfunction (aka choking). The belief not matching the want can definitely lead to a false start or never really picking that major in college. Both are kind of the same. Dissonance is how the prizefighter explains his loss: "I was fighting off the flu a week before the fight." This is how the (the same) prizefighter explains his win: "Because I was fighting the flu a week before, I lost the weight I needed while still maintaining my strength. It also put me in the fighting mind-set!" The brain wants to make things match up.

Things MUST match up. Successful people, *truly* successful people, recognize the sweet science of gratitude, belief, and discontent. They have come to terms with the fact that they may not be as happy as they would like at moments along the way. But they also know on a much deeper level that those moments of frustration or discontent are transient. They use cognitive dissonance to their advantage by resetting the bar just out of reach each time they approach it. The brain itself won't "let it go" until things line up just right. Champions talk themselves into winning rather than excusing why they shouldn't try at all. The best would rather fail at an attempt than make no attempts at all. The pain of not going for it is the real loss. This is the balance sheet of the winner.

The Balanced Life Fallacy: It's All Just *Stuff*

Who doesn't want their children to be well rounded?

Who doesn't want to live a balanced life? Articles, blogs, and entire industries are devoted to providing us "tools" to live a more balanced and fulfilled life. As a psychologist, I have witnessed and treated just as much stress (and illness) generated from efforts at creating balance as I have depression and anxiety.

Balance is not about keeping things stable. It's about being balanced when things are unstable. Those who have the luxury of thinking about a balanced life and what that looks like for them have usually accumulated and earned a certain level of status and assets and a group of friends and family. They have things they value and do not want to lose. Yet there is a perceived and, perhaps, inherent risk in taking on new ventures or moving toward new goals.

Energy is spent avoiding the stuff we don't want. It's as if we are on a teeter-totter. Every time we move toward the stuff we want, the stuff we don't want comes sliding down from the other end toward us. To keep the stuff we don't want at bay, we back off. Much energy is spent avoiding and/or looking behind us as we inch our way forward.

Being stuck takes a lot of energy

When you commit to moving decisively toward what you want, the stuff you don't want will follow. However, you will also get closer to the things you're after. When you eventually get what you want, the stuff you don't want may catch up. Hell, the stuff you don't want may hit you and push you toward the stuff you do want!

As we move toward our goals, the stuff we don't want may follow

Would you rather have the stuff you want while dealing with the things you don't, rather than deal with the stuff you don't want and *not* have the stuff you want? Pause for a moment, and give that some thought—reread the last few lines, if it helps. Moving toward a clear goal or destination puts you on a more solid foundation to deal with the instabilities of life.

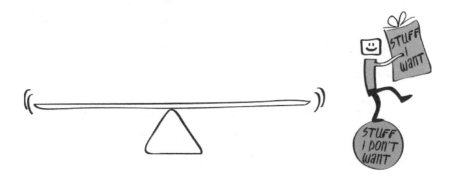

It is much easier to deal with the stuff we don't want when we have the stuff we do want

Goals/Wants/Expectations

Having purpose places us on solid ground. The clearer the purpose (goal), the easier it will be for the brain to recruit the necessary circuitry and ancillary actions to get the job(s) done. Consciously working toward and refining your goals/wants/expectations is a habit worth forming.

Goals and wants are often the same thing. However, when working with clients, I ask that they set their wants above their goals and use their goals as mile markers toward earning their wants. If you want to graduate with high honors, what will be your goals on the way to achieving this? The reason I advise people to create this hierarchy is because of the importance of language (which will be addressed in more detail later). *Wants* speak to a more primal part of the brain than goals—especially if the goals are not necessarily your own. So working to define what you want and why is important when lining up your goals and expectations.

When I ask about expectations, things definitely begin to go sideways. Even those who do expect to perform well sometimes won't admit it. I'm fine with them not wanting to admit it to others, as being humble or respectful is a virtue. We all have an internal crystal ball, and it's fuzzy at best. Publicly or outwardly predicting future events can cause uneasiness when we're put on the spot. "Will you win the event?" Who really knows? We get on the line to find out! "Can you win?" "Do you think you will meet your goals?" Shifting your expectations to *you in your process,* versus focusing solely on the result, will make lining up your wants, goals, and expectations much easier for your brain to achieve. This will also help minimize some of the detours on your journey.

Why Versus How

People tend to get caught up on *how.* Generally speaking, I can best tell you how something's done *after* it has been done! It's a hindsight thing, which is why we have things such as earthquake engineering, amber alerts, or natural history museums. How we came to be is vital to our continued growth, and we should become students of our history.

My father is a contractor in Las Vegas. Schools, parks, fire stations, and casinos are all built following a very detailed set of plans or blueprints, the "how" if you will. As detailed as these specifications are, there can still be setbacks. The unforeseen can slow the job down and even threaten completion. Sometimes the blueprints themselves become outdated by the time the contract has been awarded because a specified material is no longer available. If materials are available, the project is still subject to fabrication delays and/or long delivery times, at which point paperwork follows informing the architects, clients, and inspectors of the issue in order to get the right people to approve or extend timelines. The best and most detailed "how" can be sabotaged at any given moment.

Yet the project is completed anyway because there's a whole host of "whys" superseding the "hows." The kids need more classrooms. Neighborhoods need fire protection. People want their gambling and drinking fix a certain way! All of the reasons why a project is happening are more important than how it will get done. The "why" motivates us to find or create solutions. The why gives meaning to the thing we are doing. Incidentally, I called my dad to get clarification on this issue—he was in his motor home fixing something that probably didn't need to be fixed. After our conversation, I asked him point blank, "Has there ever been a project that wasn't completed or that you delivered late?" He answered, quicker than I could finish the question, "All

**of our jobs are completed on time and never declared late!"
Why? He wants to enjoy his new motor home with his
grandchildren!**

As you move forward, get reacquainted with *why* you
work so hard and why you do the things you like to do. If you
are hard pressed to find any meaning or reasons, you may have
found the answer to why you are not moving forward.

Action Items with Dr. Rob Irwin, Ph.D.

What would all this challenging of thoughts and
perceptions mean without any action? In the chain (beliefs
→feelings → actions → results) illustrated in Chapter Seven,
actions are most independent. Meaning, in *your control.*

1. **What DO YOU want?** Ask yourself often what it is you
    want in work, play, and life. Get used to asking big
    questions of yourself AND defining or refining your
    wants. Be as specific as you can with this. You and your
    brain will appreciate it along the way. Clear messages
    are usually delivered more efficiently.

2. **Reach** for two things: a) the thing you know and see
    yourself doing/getting, and b) the thing you really want
    but struggle with thinking is possible. Start with both!
    There is value in achieving a goal (the first thing), and
    there is value in pushing yourself beyond what you have
    done before (the second thing). Both will pay off.

3. **Write it down**. Writing things down makes our brains work in a specific and directed manner. It forces our brains to make sense of all the thoughts floating around in our heads. As soon as our thoughts hit paper, they become real. Think of this exercise as a dress rehearsal minus the stage and costumes. Mike Day's Olympic account was surreal because he lived it in his mind before he actually experienced it by writing those wants and goals down on paper![46]

4. **Set a timeline**. A timeframe allows your nonconscious brain to understand what you're doing because your nonconscious brain is extremely literal; it does not do well at interpreting vagueness. Setting a date for completion allows your nonconscious brain to go to work. Remember, the discomfort between where you are and where you want to be can HELP you meet the challenge.

5. **Measure, quantify, and qualify.** Find a way to track your progress: pounds on a scale, speed, time, and unsolicited or solicited opinion. Let the metrics *only* serve as a guide. It is easy to base our mood and worth on such measurements. We are all more than our

---

[46] The real story is how he made the Olympic team. I was actively competing that year with and against him. Everyone "knew" he was going to win the Olympic trials, and it started with him, his belief, and his plan, though he was open to getting to the big show in other ways such as being coach's pick or leading the point series through the selections process.

measurements. Learn to read between the lines. Sometimes we step back before we make bigger gains.

You may already be there:

Dr. Irwin has conducted hundreds of seminars, and one of the most common goals of attendees is "I want to be financially independent." One attendee was a woman who made $400,000 in profit by selling her home. Instead of reinvesting it into real estate, she rolled her money into an account where she felt she could make 7 percent on the principal. She took the roughly $30,000 a year as her living wage. She dropped her living expenses way down—renting a small room for six months of the year and staying/living with friends or family for the other six months. She bartered, traded, and picked up odd jobs (and experiences) if she wanted to generate more income. This woman was very clear about what financial freedom meant to her. Had she not taken the time to measure, quantify, and qualify her goal, how would she have known when she reached her point of independence? I just hope she didn't wear out her welcome with family and friends.

6. **Rule in rather than rule out.** Many times we give ourselves only one way to win. I have worked with many sprinters who thought they always had to be the fastest off the blocks to win. During competition, you could see the same person shut down (mentally and physically) if they didn't get the start they wanted. But, who is to say

the people in front are going to run a perfect race? If you shut down, how are you able capitalize on the leaders' mistakes? Keep applying pressure. The odds do not dictate the outcome. When drawing your blueprint for success, leave room for the unexplained, unplanned, and downright silly dumb luck. Being open to such anomalies allows you to cash in on them. Ruling out ways to meet your goal might get you from point A to point B. Ruling in other possibilities will get you from point A to point Z.

7. **Recalibrate with language**. Apple's "Think Different" campaign of the late 1990s was powerful, though not because it changed the public's image of Apple (although it did). It was powerful because it changed Apple's image of Apple. Actually, it *enhanced* Apple's image of itself at a time it needed it most. Grammatically, "Think Different" missuses an adjective. Verbal commands need adverbs (think differently), but because it's a slogan, language is used to convey an idea and sell a product. From a belief system standpoint, "Think Perfect!"

Words have weight. Using phrases such as "have to," "got to," and "need to" are like adding weights to the already heavy loads we lift. Referring to our past with words like "woulda," "coulda," and "shoulda" shackle us to our past failures. The words "will" and "going" both beg the question, "When?"

Rules are already in place for every game we play, and there are laws for every facet of life. The things you have to, got to, and need to do are implicit in the game. Ultimately, if you choose to play, it's because you want to, like to, and can. Rather than would, could, or should, let's just say, "haven't yet," or "learned to/learned not to." Can you do that? Before you answer, remember "I am" is much more powerful than "I will" or "I'm going to." If you must use "will" or "going to," specify when you will and when you are going to. There is a big difference between saying, "I will take out the trash" and "I am taking out the trash." "Don't hit that rock" is much harder to calibrate than "Stay on course." Your brain, your parents, and/or your spouse will thank you for it later! Now if you have children, speaking in an affirmative way all the time is a difficult task. "Hands to your sides" may work better than "Don't touch the fire," but you're forgiven if you say the latter!

8. **Keep your eyes on the ball.** Write and rewrite your wants, goals, and expectations often. Read them. Post them on your mirror by your toothbrush. Place them in your car. Have your phone alert you of them every day. There was a reason Rocky placed a picture of Drago on his mirror in Rocky IV!

9. **Slow down to go faster and/or further.** See yourself be yourself. What do we see athletes do before they step in to the batter's box or the starting blocks before game time? What do stage actors do just before the curtain goes up? We have all seen it. They pause,

sometimes closing their eyes, and take deep breaths. They slow themselves down to do what they intend to do. It only takes a few seconds. Why don't we do this everyday when switching tasks, pulling in the driveway, getting to the office, or talking to our children? The milliseconds we save rushing and reacting is time gone by unnoticed. The seconds it takes to breathe and see ourselves doing what we set out to do—big or small, macro or micro—is time added when we are aware and engaged. In other words, the way to self-medicate is to *meditate*.[47]

10. **Time is your friend.** Time is on your side. Use it to your advantage. This doesn't mean stuffing everything into every minute. It means intentionally working toward something. It means making decisions. How would you become a lawyer if you did not go to law school or even apply? Whether you choose to act or not, the years will pass. If you can say that you would rather be a lawyer in three to seven years than not at all, get to work! Results are for those who act. Consequences are for those who don't.

11. **Challenge yourself.** Drive a different way home today. Brush your teeth with the opposite hand. Ask for feedback from your worst critics! Write down three things you want to accomplish today and *do* them! Join

---

[47] http://www.emmaseppala.com/10-science-based-reasons-start-meditating-today-infographic/#.VMnbrMa6eXQ

a group. Commit to a thirty, sixty, or ninety-day challenge—with people who will hold you accountable. Go veggie. Go vegan. Go paleo. Go high carb, slow carb, no carb . . . just *GO!*[48]

12. **Gratitude adjustment.** Learn to take pleasure in seeing other people get what they want. Even when you compete, be happy for those who win. Your feelings about a specific result don't have to be a measure of how you feel about yourself. That guy who won may be the guy helping you get better.

13. **Invest.** What's the biggest difference between amateur and pro? Usually, both have the same potential. Some amateurs even show more potential than the pros show ability. However, there are two differences. The pro executes on cue *and* in the heat of the moment. Amateurs (sometimes masquerading as pros) can only perform as long as there is nothing on the line. The other difference is the pro has everything on the line. They're invested more than everyone else. Time, effort, money, and yes, even pieces of your sanity may be required in order to achieve what you want.

14. **Hire your boss.** The best have someone in their corner looking out for their best interests. It may take some time to find this person. Or it might make sense to have several "bosses" for your work, play, and life. It's not

---

[48] This is not an endorsement or recommendation for any specific diet or training regime. It is however, an endorsement for changing behavior.

about ego because in the end you are doing the hiring. Having someone who cares keep you sharp is good for you and your endeavors. Consider this exercise a "good investment" in accountability.

15. **Pay yourself first.** Responsible people meet the daily demands of work and life. Unfortunately, we can be responsible at the expense of our own well-being or integration of better habits. Prioritize your investment resources—time, money, and effort—for the things you say you've wanted to do but never seemed to get around to do. Some of those things you've been putting off may help you in ways you have yet to imagine. Since, I am guessing, you *are* responsible – you paying yourself first *is* the responsible action. There is a reason airlines want parents to put their masks on first: Dead people don't save anyone.

It would be hypocritical to tell you that you *have* to do all the things on the list. Dr. Irwin and I are not telling you to do these things. We are hoping you *want* to do these things. The action items are not meant to be more "stuff you gotta do." They only take a moment, and a moment is all it takes. We trust that given enough practice (and thought), you'll end up doing some of these things automatically.

Chapter 12

The Market: It's Bigger Than You

"Yet, the project gets done anyway because there's a whole host of 'whys' superseding the 'hows.'"

Understand that setting out to live your dream, to be the best, stake your claim, or whatever cliché you prefer does not guarantee fame and fortune even when you attain mastery. Our world is shrinking as more and more people fill it with ideas, products, and services. Somehow, as the world becomes smaller, it seems we are compelled to speak louder. Even the most famous among us shout, scream, and yell at times to be noticed. Then, once noticed, we all move on to the next #trending topic. Attention is short.

Staging pictures of your dinner/gym session/feet in the sand with the appropriate #hashtags seems to be the skill du jour as everyone is now a "brand" unto themselves. Everyone's selling and everyone's buying. Heck, tell your story well enough, and you'll either become co-opted, crowdfunded, or both. The market, in economical, ideological, and countless other forms is diluted, vast, impacted, and still untapped—and *that* is an understatement.

I grew up in a sport that was, and still is, growing up. I was also fortunate enough to capitalize on a second resurgence of the sport. The guys who found themselves routinely scraping together pennies for gas money became (multiple) homeowners. We compared investments as much as we compared who beat whom at the World Cup. Our miles earned flying to events was at times more of a status symbol than how many titles we earned from the events. It was a race to get to the first class cabin just as much as it was to get to the finish line. It was ridiculous, but at the same time, some of the best times in our lives. For a ragtag group of twenty-somethings, we did very well, and the average person had no idea about the sport or the top pros in it.

As most humans do, some of us couldn't help but look over our proverbial fence. We compared our level of pay to other athletes in mainstream sports (think: baseball, basketball, football). We may have worked just as hard as any mainstream athlete. We definitely traveled as much. However, our names

were only known within our specific market. We weren't
mobbed at airports like WWE wrestlers or NBA players, who fly
charter or fly in private planes.[49] It was our choice to get on the
bikes and make our mark by racing them. Athleticism and work
ethic aside, the market dictated our level of pay. Or was it our
market reach?

The wakeup call came in 2003 when a few of us were
invited to the US Olympic Training Center in Colorado Springs
for "testing." The coaching staff at USA Cycling wanted to see if
our sprinting talent would cross over to track (velodrome)
cycling.[50] We were all amazed at how hard velodrome racers
worked and how little they received in remuneration. They lived
in dorms and paid for their own equipment, and the prize
money available to them barely covered dinner and a movie for
two. Meanwhile, the track cyclists were amazed at how good we
had it. To those guys, we were mainstream. They couldn't
believe how much we made or the fact that we didn't have to
pay for any of our equipment. The market, again, dictated their
level of (non)compensation. Ironically, as a group, made up of

---

[49] McCartney, Scott., *Teams Score Elite Service in the Sky*:
http://www.wsj.com/articles/SB1000142405297020389740457807657412 64
94236
[50] One of our peers, "Sir" Jamie Staff, had already done this for his home
country. He moved to the US from Great Britain to race BMX; he crossed
over to track cycling and won silver at the Olympics in Athens and gold in
Beijing. He is currently director of BMX for USA Cycling. Also, Jamie was
compensated much more handsomely in Great Britain as a track cyclist than
we could have been in the US as track cyclists. Again, the market was in
play.

both cycling disciplines, we matched the performance level of any top elite athlete from any sport.

Back when I was racing and in college, I visited my family in Vegas and we decided to go to a casino for breakfast (no, not a buffet). We all got in the elevator, and the last person in was a very famous movie star/former "Saturday Night Live" cast member. I recognized him straightaway, and it wasn't until he walked out that my younger sister realized who he was. She was only in junior high at the time. At breakfast she carried on like any star-struck teenager. She couldn't believe what had just happened.

I was a bit annoyed with her to be honest. Usually, she revered me! I get it, though. He was rich, famous, and on TV and had several box office hits. Seeing the person you watch on TV stand in front of you in real life is a bit surreal and does carry its own special cachet.

In my annoyance, I realized something: My sister lives in a family where her mother immigrated to the United States to become a special needs teacher, her father is an entrepreneur with several projects worth hundreds of thousands to millions of dollars, and her brother is a pro athlete. Yet we were just another family having breakfast. So what about the table next to us? And the table next to the table next to us? It occurred to me that excellence could exist everywhere regardless of size, perceived status, or pay grade. That's a good thing! Fame does not equate to

greatness or accomplishment and vice versa. This puts a whole new spin on what it means to compete!

BMX racing has been an Olympic sport for two Olympiads going on three come Rio 2016. That either means it has hit the big time and has arrived, or it means it is on the fringe and obscure, like curling. I tend to think it's a bit of both. This is the point: The famous person in the elevator chose a discipline within a market where, if you are immensely talented, more people notice and/or pay more for the talent. The current BMX athlete chose something that only fills some smaller arenas in Europe and South America, whereas it competes with baseball, hotdogs, and apple pie in the States.

Over a decade after "the breakfast"—my wife's boss has a friend who worked for NFL Films as one of the lead filmmakers. For fun, her boss would go to the games with his friend and help by carrying extra equipment, keeping cords out of the way, and so on. I always thought it was funny; I'm sure some of the players looked at this middle-aged guy and thought he was just some poor schlep assistant. In reality, this "poor schlep" made more than the average starter and will continue to do so long after they've stopped playing! This poor schlep was actually the leader of a publicly traded company.

As stated earlier, the market is vast. And it's not all just about economics. It's about *value*. My wife's boss didn't need to score touchdowns because the market he chose to play in did not value fame or athletic prowess. The NFL players and the CEO camera assistant are actually in the same ocean; they're just riding different waves. Some break easy and offer long rides. Others peak early and have steep drops. Both offer valuable experiences; both are susceptible to the tides and swells.

When the dust settled after my retirement from racing, I couldn't help but make comparisons to those with whom I had competed. How did we all end up? How did I fare? Who's still "living the dream?" Those comparisons soon caused me to look at the athletes who preceded me more than the ones who followed. Then I looked at my neighbors, my city, my country, and so on just as I looked at the other tables during breakfast years ago. It's as if I was that guy in the old western riding the horse for days passing the same rock and tumbleweed!

In the end, drawing comparisons is pointless because none of us are finished yet. We all have many more cycles before we "end up!"

Defining the Win

Everyone deals with traffic. I'm always amazed at the self-righteousness of some people who go fifty-five mph in the fast lane and refuse to move over for faster vehicles. It's also just as silly when the slow guy catches the speeding guy at every stoplight. But who's to say your destinations are the same? If you're already in your neighborhood, there is no reason to speed. If you have a long way to go and a short time to get there[51], then speed might be your friend, even if it's not practical during all points in the journey.

In 2012, I was asked to speak at a coaching certification training program at the US Olympic Training Center in Chula Vista, CA. Communication and goals were a major portion of my presentation, and in my presentation I said, "Your athletes may not be there to win." This confounded some of the attendees. "What do you mean?" one coach asked. "Why else would they be there?" In a place like the Olympic Training Center, that is a totally fair question to a seemingly insane statement. I answered, "Your athletes may not be there for first place. Maybe competing keeps them out of school or work—or their home. They might be in it for social reasons. They might be satisfied with just making it to the semifinals or just being competitive in general. If you are going to build a trusting and successful relationship, you are going to want to define what their win is because it may not be first place! But, if you can define the win (what they want) and work toward that, your athlete may just end up placing first anyway or be ready to do so the next time."

The continuum precedes us and extends beyond us. It's bigger than you, which is precisely why you can play as big as you want because it keeps on going. Your job is to define what it

---

[51] Who doesn't love the *Smokey and the Bandit* theme song?

is you want and believe you can do it or, at the very least, that it's *possible* for you. Then, most importantly, go after it!

You are in a different race than your neighbor. You are even in a different race than the ones with whom you compete against. After you get to the traffic light or freeway entrance, you and your neighbor go in different directions. Once you cross the finish line, you and your competitors go your separate ways. This is the *human* race. It's run on your own *and* in parallel with others. In the human race, *we* can define our wins, and we can decide where the finish lines are. Going after what you want is where the win is. So, where is it you want to go? What is it you want to do?

The journey is long, and it will be over before you know it! Choose your BS wisely.

Discretionary Bonus(es) Chapter

Work, Play, Life: Profit and Loss Statement

"We are very good at keeping our beliefs in "silos." This compartmentalization allows us to have competing beliefs, both within a given subject and among different subjects."

We often wear different hats in different arenas. In work, at play, and in life, we create separate profit and loss (P&L) statements to account for how we are doing. We keep score dutifully while in that respective arena or domain, then jump to the next P&L statement once we shift our pursuits. Usually one P&L receives more attention than others.

Life doesn't happen in silos, and the things that fill our lives often cannot be placed neatly into bento boxes. While it's important to keep track of revenue and cost, it's also important to recognize that not all the revenue comes to us in dollars and cents. Rather then keeping several P&L statements for the different aspects of our lives, why not maintain one P&L statement with several line items? Rather than looking at costs and revenue from a dollars and cents perspective, why not also account for time, satisfaction, experience, people, and relationships? These items, too, have costs and revenue associated with them.

Given the game is long and that we are on a continuum, it only follows that at different points in our journey, different things have value to us for different reasons. You may not do the next deal (just) for the money because time might be your greatest asset. The moment your child grabs your hand to cross the street might be a greater payoff than staying up late to finalize a report. The day you receive an unexpected visit from a lifelong friend *is* the Christmas bonus. Taking your kids on a road trip to surprise Mom or Dad on a work trip is an invaluable investment. The day you start work *and* the day you leave to start your own company both have immeasurable valuations. Line items such as these all lead to a profitable life.

As you take inventory of your assets, recognize your profits and losses are not limited to your job, income, or bank account. You are connected to a limitless network of people, places, and things. The only common denominator in your life is you. If you don't account for the line items where you profit the most, how will you allocate the appropriate resources?

Bonuses are always tied to performance in the (legitimate) business world. However, they are not always fixed. Bonuses in some instances are discretionary. When we take our work, play, and life in total and place them on one P&L statement, it forces us to find the discrete payoffs. You can miss profits by only looking at one spreadsheet at a time or jumping back and forth from screen to screen. Open your focus to include all of your assets, offerings, and rewards; you may find there is more *change* under the cushion than you anticipated.

Meet the Chief Belief Officers:

Rob Irwin, PhD - By DrJRich

Dr. Rob has a drive to change the world's negative beliefs to effective beliefs.

In 2009, I became this guy's intern. At the time, he was doing some of what I wanted to do. Not only was he kind enough to give me work, allowing me to complete my hours and become licensed, he included me in a seminar that he and his father, a board-certified surgeon, created. The seminars were twelve-week programs based on neuroscience with the specific goal of helping people create new neurological connections through willful thought and action. Rob's mission is to give people an evidenced-based method to discover what holds them back. He has led over 200 twelve-week programs with over 5,000 participants in total. His mission is proving to be a success!

You can find Dr. Irwin crushing a golf ball on many of North County, San Diego's finest golf courses. He lives in Vista, CA, with his wife and is the father of three children.

Connect with Dr. Rob Irwin on Twitter @DrRob1rwin

Jason Richardson, PsyD, MBA - By Mike

Carruth, editor

Every now and then, DrJRich still challenges himself where it all began.

As a professional BMX racer, Jason always looked beyond the track to build advantages that would carry him through life. Throughout his racing career, Richardson set his eyes on several finish lines, earning a BA in Philosophy in 1997, an MBA in 2000, and his doctorate in psychology in 2010, while maintaining an ambitious racing schedule during most of his academic pursuits.

In 2010, "JRich" became known as "Dr. JRich" to clients, friends, and past competitors. His unique blend of education and professional experience sets the table for a business that plays an important role in the lives of patients, clients in the corporate world, the entrepreneurial ecosystem, and the athletic field of play.

A compelling public speaker, Dr. Richardson regularly addresses audiences looking to get on top, stay on top, or break new barriers toward exceptional personal achievement. In a recent interview, Dr. JRich said, "I have always liked to write and have wanted to write a series of books long before I became a psychologist." His first title, "It's all B.S.! We're All Wrong, and You're All Right!" explores our respective belief systems (the "B.S." in the book title) in a very approachable fashion and causes the readers to ask questions of themselves that help them unlock hidden potential and move past what often holds us back in our personal and professional lives.

Dr. Richardson currently resides in Carlsbad, CA, with his wife and two sons.

Connect with DrJrich on Twitter and Instagram:

@RealDrJrich

www.drjasonrichardson.com

#ItsALLBSBook

#WELLthCycle

#WELLthManagement

#MentalWELLth

#BeyondTheGrind

CPSIA information can be obtained
at www.ICGtesting.com
Printed in the USA
FSOW03n0630180316
18088FS